A WAY OUT OF NO WAY

A Way Out of No Way

THE ECONOMIC PREREQUISITES
OF THE BELOVED COMMUNITY

Read, Enjoy & Be Blessed

Michael Greene

CASCADE *Books* · Eugene, Oregon

A WAY OUT OF NO WAY
The Economic Prerequisites of the Beloved Community

Cascade Books
An Imprint of Wipf and Stock Publishers
199 W. 8th Ave., Suite 3
Eugene, OR 97401

www.wipfandstock.com

ISBN 13: 978-1-62032-580-3

Cataloging-in-Publication data:

Greene, Michael.

A way out of no way : the economic prerequisites of the beloved community / Michael Greene.

xvi + 100 p.; 23 cm—Includes bibliographical references.

ISBN 13: 978-1-62032-580-3

1. Economics—Religious aspects—Christianity. 2. King, Martin Luther, Jr., 1929–1968—Ethics. 3. King, Martin Luther, Jr., 1929–1968—Political and social views. 4. Darity, William A., 1953–. 5. Harvey, Philip, 1946-. I. Title.

E185.97.K5 G74 2014

Manufactured in the USA.

Contents

Introduction

Is It Really Over?

Okay, let me make sure I've got this straight: the Great Recession is over, right? Well, at least that's what we've been told by those whose job it is to monitor fluctuations in the nation's business cycle. In fact, the National Bureau of Economic Research (NBER)—that private group of prestigious economists who "date" the beginnings of recessions and recoveries—notes that this most recent recession began in December 2007 and officially ended in June 2009, a period of eighteen months. At the time of this writing (May 2012), then, the folks at the NBER would have us believe that not only is the Great Recession over, but—and this might be a bit hard for some to swallow—it's been over for almost three years.

Despite the official ending of the Great Recession—a long-lasting and painful "event" in which the economy shed some eight million jobs—millions still find themselves stuck in an economic quagmire. Like who? Well, for starters, how about the 12.5 million unemployed persons? Or, if that doesn't get your dander up, how about throwing in the mix the one million "discouraged" workers who, because of our anemic labor markets, have gotten frustrated, thrown in the towel, and dropped out of the labor force? Just in case you're counting, that's over twenty million people who probably roll their eyes and shake their heads in disbelief every time a politician or a talking head proclaims that "it" is finally over.

Rising Poverty, Falling Earnings, and Vanishing Health Care Coverage

Jobs are absolutely essential to most people's economic security. An economy that fails to produce a sufficient number of jobs is an economy that will be characterized by growing numbers of person enmeshed in poverty and without health care coverage. So, we shouldn't be surprised that the Great Recession—and the tepid recovery that followed its official ending—contributed to rising poverty, falling earnings, and vanishing health care coverage. But, at the very least, we ought to be disturbed—if not outright angry. Later on I'll talk about some of the ways in which we can channel these emotions to make things better. For the moment, check yourself to see how angry or disturbed you get at the following:

- Between 2008 and 2009—years covered by the Great Recession—the number of people in poverty jumped from 39.8 to 43.6 million. In terms of percentages, the current poverty rate is 14.3 percent, up from 13.2 percent in 2008.

- Between 2007—the year before the onset of the Great Recession—and 2009, the number of persons in poverty increased by a whopping 6.3 million. And the number of children in poverty increased by 2.1 million.

- If communities of color have been slammed by job loss, they've been slapped by poverty increases. Between 2008 and 2009, the poverty rate for Whites increased from 8.6 percent to 9.4 percent; for Africans-Americans, from 24.7 percent to 25.8 percent; and for Latinos, from 23.2 percent to 25.2 percent.

That's a lot of numbers. For starters, take the number of persons in poverty. If we were to "grant" those forty-four million persons their own geographical territory, they would constitute the largest state in the union, exceeding the 2010 population of California by several million persons. And if that doesn't trouble you, then ponder this: one out of every four persons of color is below the poverty line.

Now, here's the skinny on those other two things I mentioned earlier—earnings and health care coverage. Just in case your eyes are starting to glaze over, I'll keep it brief (or at least I'll try to do so):[1]

- Between 2007 and 2009, the real median earnings of male workers declined from $37,898 to $36,331, a drop of about 4.1 percent. For women, median earnings went from $26,770 to $26,030, a 2.8 percent drop.

- The number of men and women without earnings jumped during the Great Recession. Over the 2007–2009 period, the number of males reporting zero earnings increased by 2.5 million; for women, zero earners increased by 1.3 million.

- During the 2008–2009 period, the percentage of persons covered by employment-based health insurance declined from 58.5 percent to 55.8 percent. That 55.8 percent marks the lowest percentage of persons covered by employment-based insurance since such data was first collected in 1987.

- Between 2008 and 2009, the number of Whites lacking health insurance increased by 1.2 percent, from about 21.3 to 23.7 million. For African-Americans, the increase was 1.8 percent, as the number of uninsured Blacks jumped from 7.3 to 8.1 million. Currently, 15.8 percent of Whites and 21 percent of African-Americans lack health coverage.

- The withering of employment-based health insurance is really hurting African-Americans. Only 45 percent of African-Americans are currently covered by employment-based insurance, down from 50 percent in 2007. In contrast, about 73 percent of Whites are covered by some form of employment-based insurance, although even this is down from the 2007 figure of 75 percent.

---

1. The statistics in this section come from Bivens, *Failure by Design*, 13–28.

- Latinos are getting slammed real hard by the decreasing availability of employment-based health care coverage. Only 3.7 out of every ten Hispanics are covered by such insurance, down from four out of every ten in 2007.

So, there you have it: millions are getting slammed by job losses, slapped by increases in poverty, and snatched from the roles of the insured. Slammed, slapped, and snatched—and, yes, communities of color are getting whacked especially hard.

Unslammed, Unslapped, and Unsnatched

What we really need is to get unslammed, unslapped, and unsnatched. However, that's not likely to happen anytime soon unless we undertake some pretty bold policy initiatives. I say this for several reasons. First, remember that, although officially over, the Great Recession's job slide was long and hard: As of May 2011, we were still down about 6.9 million jobs, with another 4.1 million needed just to accommodate the growth in new labor-market entrants. That's eleven million jobs needed just to get the job market back to its prerecession health. If that sounds like a big number to you, you're right—and, again, we're unlikely to recapture that lost ground soon unless we summon up the moral courage needed to do something and to do it quick. You'll hear more about that "something" in subsequent chapters. For the moment, given the tepid pace of the recovery—a measly fifty-four thousand new jobs added in May 2011—trying to wait this thing out is a sure-fire recipe for prolonging misery for millions. As economist Josh Bivens observes, *"[I]t could well be a decade or more before the pre-recession unemployment rate is restored* unless policy makers take more aggressive steps to jumpstart the economy."[2] Indeed, the Congressional Budget Office projects that the unemployment rate will not decline to 5 percent until 2016.[3]

2. Bivens, *Failure by Design*, 7. Bivens' italics.
3. Congressional Budget Office, *Budget and Economic Outlook*, 25.

The need for action is further underscored by recent data on the ratio of job seekers to job vacancies. Consider this: there are about five job seekers for every job vacancy—meaning that for large numbers of unemployed persons there are simply no jobs to be had. You can't expect people to get themselves unslammed, unslapped, and unsnatched if the means to do so are not available—or at least not sufficiently available. Hey, I've got nothing against personal responsibility, and, quite frankly, I believe that work is one of the ways in which everyone can contribute to the meeting of human needs and to the common good. But it's one thing to scream "Get a job!" to folks when the economy is producing employment opportunities at a breakneck pace; it's quite another thing to insist that the jobless find work when the economy is not generating sufficient employment opportunities for them. When the ratio of job seekers to job vacancies is running somewhere in the neighborhood of five to one, only the most callous would argue that the problem is one of character flaws or moral defects on the part of the jobless. What we're really dealing with is an abysmal failure on the part of the economy to provide decent jobs and employment security to large swaths of the population.

Lastly, urgent action is needed because it is getting harder and harder for the jobless to dig themselves out of the depths of unemployment. I already mentioned how our current job gap—the discrepancy between job seekers and job vacancies—hampers the ability of the jobless to secure employment. To add insult to injury, growing percentages of the jobless are falling into that unenviable category of "long-term unemployed." And just who are these folks? Well, first off, let's take the definition used by the federal government. According to the feds, you fall into that category if you've been jobless for at least twenty-seven weeks. As of May 2011—the most recent data available at the time of this writing—about 45 percent of the jobless had been unemployed for at least twenty-seven weeks, up from 43.4 percent just one month earlier (April 2011). So, of the roughly fourteen million unemployed persons, 6.2 million of them have been jobless for at least twenty-seven weeks.

But there's another insightful way of grasping the problem of long-term unemployment—namely, getting a grip on the percentage of the unemployed who have been jobless for at least a year (if six months is bad, a year is obviously worse). A report by the Pew Economic Policy Group, titled "A Year or More: The High Cost of Long-Term Unemployment," does just that. Using data from the December 2009 Current Population Survey, Pew researchers found that approximately 23 percent of the unemployed had been jobless for a least a year. In raw numbers, that's about 3.4 million people, a figure that approximates the size of the state of Connecticut.[4] More recently, Pew researchers found that during the first quarter of 2012, approximately 30 percent of the unemployed had been jobless for a least a year—a figure that translates into almost four million persons and that is equivalent to the population of the state of Oregon.[5] Whether we peg it at six months or a year, this much is clear: long-term unemployment is more than long enough to lose a home, to have a vehicle repossessed, to strain a marriage to the breaking point, or to erode one's self-esteem. It's bad enough to have millions of persons jobless; it's downright deplorable when millions of those millions have to suffer the indignity of being without employment indefinitely.

Core Thesis and Methodology

This book is about how we can dig ourselves out of our current economic mess—that is, how we can begin the process of getting unslammed, unslapped, and unsnatched. As an exercise in Christian social ethics, its central thesis is that by rediscovering, retrieving, and reassessing the economic prerequisites of Martin Luther King, Jr.'s beloved community, the church in general—and the

4. Pew Economic Policy Group, "A Year or More," 3. The Pew Fiscal Analysis Initiative, a division of the Pew Economic Policy Group, released the report in April 2010.

5. Pew Economic Policy Group, "Addendum—A Year or More," 1. This addendum, released in May 2012, is an update of the 2010 report referenced above.

Black church in particular—can (*a*) make a significant contribution to public discourse about the causes and cures of our current economic crisis, and (*b*) proffer a way out of the joblessness and impoverishment that continues to plague the land. More specifically, I contend that at the heart of King's beloved community is a robust conception of full employment that incorporates both a quantitative and qualitative dimension—that is, for King, genuine full employment obtains when there are enough jobs at livable wages to employ all those who are able, ready, and willing to work. For King, then, the struggle for social and economic justice is part and parcel of the struggle to secure genuine full employment.

This book stands out from the extant literature on King by, first of all, bringing him into conversation with a school of economic thought that is acutely concerned, as was King, with the securing of economic, racial, and social justice. While not necessarily sharing King's theological views, this school of thought nevertheless calls for a massive jobs program that bears a striking resemblance to King's own clarion call for an economic bill of rights. By allowing King to enter into conversation with this school of economic thought, I show how his basic economic analysis is enriched when allowed to interact with a more mature or developed understanding of exactly what it will cost to secure full employment and realize the right to work—both of which, as I argue, constitute the basic economic prerequisites of King's conception of the beloved community. This conversation also aids us in assessing and appreciating the contemporary relevance of the economic prerequisites of the beloved community.

Secondly, by drawing upon the work of a couple of progressive economists, this texts seeks to correct what I'd argue is a serious defect in King' proposed economic bill of rights. Specifically, the dialogical approach employed in this study enables me to demonstrate how one might go about rebutting the claim of detractors that, while laudable, efforts to bring to fruition the economic prerequisites of the beloved community will do more harm than good. To anticipate one of their objections, detractors often argue that the instantiation of genuine full employment and the right to work—the heart of the economic prerequisites of King's beloved community—is too costly, and, if we attempt it, we'll end up paying the price in the form of a further ballooning of the federal deficit and higher rates of inflation. In contrast, I'll suggest that the "price of the ticket" is not nearly as high as commonly assumed; we can, I'll argue, implement King's economic bill of rights in a way that does not add appreciably—if at all—to the federal debt and that does not lead to an unmanageable inflationary spiral. I make no pretense to having demolished all the possible claims that detractors might lodge against King's policy prescriptions for the eradication of involuntary joblessness and its attendant ills. Still, undercutting the argument that the price of the ticket is too high, makes this text, I believe, worthy in and of itself.

The Takeaway Point

All authors have—or should have—a takeaway point. So you might be wondering, what's mine? Quite simply this: if those of us who admire King truly wish to honor him, then we must assiduously engage in the arduous task of completely wiping out involuntary joblessness and poverty. To do this will require more than printing his face on stamps, erecting marble monuments to him, and acquiescing to annual calls for a "day of service." Stamps, monuments, and annual "days of service" cannot promote and protect human dignity—they cannot, that is, rearrange out current socioeconomic configurations such that human flourishing is no longer stifled by economic marginality.

Now, don't get me wrong; what follows is not a diatribe against stamps, monuments, and service. I'd be the last one to argue that these symbolic gestures are meaningless. But to borrow a common phrase in the African-American community, I've "got enough sense to know" that, in the final analysis, you can't eat marble and you sure as hell can't pay your basic necessities with stamps. And, what's more, I've "got enough sense to know" that there's a world of a difference between a "day of service," on the one hand, and social, racial, and economic justice, on the other. My hope is that after reading this text, you too will agree that destiny does not consign us to make peace with social and economic arrangements that allow millions to languish in idleness and hopelessness. As moral agents we can choose "something else." And, fundamentally, this book is about that something else.

1

Revisiting the New Deal's Full-Employment/ Right-to-Work Agenda

The introduction highlighted some of the basic dimensions of joblessness and economic marginality. This chapter builds on the introduction by revisiting a particular conception of full employment that took root and began to blossom during the New Deal. This conception draws a tight connection between that particular conception of full employment and economic rights, including the right to a job with a decent wage. More particularly, the chapter has two purposes. First, it lays the groundwork for my subsequent argument that, in a very important sense, King's own theological and ethical reasoning leads him to critically reclaim the full-employment/right-to-work agenda that is characteristic of the New Deal era and to place it at the center of the economic foundations of his conception of the beloved community. Second, I draw on the work of Philip Harvey—an economist and a leading proponent of the right to work—to indicate some of the reasons why progressive economists have lost faith in the achievability of the full-employment/right-to-work agenda. Harvey's arguments are helpful, then, in viewing King from yet another angle—as an indefatigable champion who fights to the end to revitalize and realize faith in the achievability of the full-employment/right-to-work agenda.

Given the foregoing, then, an appropriate starting point for this chapter is to briefly delve into how, during the New Deal, progressives conceived of the interplay between full employment and the right to work.

A Progressive Conception of Full Employment

Let's start this section by taking a quick quiz. Take a moment and complete the following sentence: "Full employment is . . ." Now, if you've been hanging out with a bunch of economists, you'd probably complete the sentence by saying something like, "Full employment is the lowest level of joblessness compatible with price stability." Or, if you're really feeling your oats, you might get fancy and say something like, "Full employment is the non-accelerating inflation rate of unemployment." Or, taking yet another stab, you might find words like the following coming out of your mouth: "Full employment is determined by the intersection of the supply and demand for labor."

Now, none of the aforementioned answers is likely to get you tossed out of an economics class, and those economists with whom you've been hanging out would probably still welcome your company. But it's also possible that you might find the aforementioned answers a bit obtuse and off the mark. And, assuming that you felt that way, you might proffer the following answer to our brief quiz: "Full employment is that situation where jobs at decent pay are available for all those who are ready, willing, and able to work." And if that was your answer, you'd have tapped into an understanding of full employment that began to take root among those progressives who formulated the New Deal. Indeed, scholars such as William P. Quigley locate the "seeds" of this full-employment/ right-to-work linkage in the New Deal itself:

> The seeds of modern hopes for a right to a job that pays a living wage were planted in the New Deal. The federal government made great effort to safeguard and create jobs for all Americans at a time when the need was great and the opposition fierce. These actions went forward on two fronts in the New Deal: the creation of public programs providing jobs for the unemployed

and a continuing push for the creation of a right to a job for all Americans.[1]

To apprehend the importance of these "two fronts," it is critical to bear in mind the absolute economic and social catastrophe that characterized the Great Depression. Here's a brief litany:[2]

- Between 1929 and 1932, the nation's unemployment rate skyrocketed from 3 percent to 25 percent. Stated somewhat differently, the number of unemployed persons went through the roof, from 1.5 million in 1929 to between thirteen and fifteen million by the spring of 1932.

- In just four years, from 1929 to 1933, national income took a mind-boggling nosedive, plummeting from $75 billion to $40 billion.

- Incomes from wages and salaries—the very type of income that the vast majority of us need to get by—followed an identical trend, dropping from $50.8 billion in 1929 to $29.3 billion in 1933.

- Banks were closing like crazy and depositors found themselves at risk of having their funds disappear in a cloud of smoke: between 1929 and 1933, the number of banks in the United States decreased by ten thousand, from twenty-five thousand to fifteen thousand.

- The system of economic relief was essentially a joke—and a bad one at that. In 1932, for instance, only 25 percent of those eligible for assistance were able to get it. Or, looking at it from the flip side, 75 percent of those eligible to receive assistance weren't able to get as much as a dime's worth of help.

The economic and social catastrophe evident in this data was prima facie evidence of the human misery that is invariably associated with the existence of unmet human needs. Animated by the vision of such social workers as Harry Hopkins and Aubrey

1. Quigley, *Ending Poverty*, 103.

2 The data in this section come from Sunstein, *Second Bill of Rights*, 36–38.

Williams, the New Deal progressives, first and foremost, called for the direct provision of jobs for those caught knee-deep in the quicksand of unemployment and underemployment. Underlying their approach was the deep belief that the economically marginalized want and need jobs, not handouts. In fact, they were convinced that being on the dole slowly nibbled away at the self-esteem of those who desired employment but hadn't been able to secure it. Thus, in his 1935 State of the Union address, President Roosevelt argued that "continued dependence upon relief induces a spiritual disintegration fundamentally destructive to the national fiber. To dole out relief in this way is to administer a narcotic, a subtle destroyer of the human spirit. . . . Work must be found for able-bodied but destitute workers."[3] In other words, the New Deal progressives maintained that the first order of the day was the provision of jobs to protect people from the ravages of joblessness, with "relief" being reserved for those unable or not expected to participate in the paid labor market. The well-known result of all of this, of course, was a slew of public employment projects designed to meet the urgent need for jobs. These projects included the Works Progress Administration (WPA), the Civil Works Administration (CWA), and the Federal Emergency Relief Administration (FERA). Economist Nancy E. Rose reminds us that, through these three programs, "work was provided each month for 1.4 to 3.3 million people—and 4.4 million at the height of the CWA."[4] She goes on to observe that

> Payments were based on private sector wage rates. And a wide variety of socially useful projects were undertaken throughout the country. These included construction and repair of more than 200,000 public buildings, parks, and other recreational facilities, and more than a million miles of roads. In addition, people taught classes, conducted surveys, produced garments and canned produce for other relief families, and served school lunches to needy children. And there was more

3. Cited in Sunstein, *Second Bill of Rights*, 45.
4. Rose, *Put to Work*, 10.

generous government support for the arts than at any other time in history.[5]

Yet another economist, Paul Davidson, offers this reminder: "The New Deal was also responsible for building New York's Lincoln Tunnel and Triborough Bridge, a significant portion of Chicago's Lakefront, the Montana state Capitol, the Cathedral of Learning in Pittsburgh, and worthy projects that are still in use today. It also rebuilt the nation's rural school system."[6]

Not only did the New Dealers advocate in favor of public employment programs to launch a frontal attack on joblessness, but, equally important, they were also skeptical of the ability of the market, left to its own devices, to ensure the existence of genuine full employment—to ensure, that is, that all persons desiring employment would be able to secure decent jobs. Accordingly, they often equated full employment with the right to work, with the federal government functioning as the employer of last resort. Should the private sector prove incapable of providing enough jobs to wipe out involuntary joblessness, it would then become the duty of the feds to provide or guarantee the much-needed jobs to secure the full-employment/right-to-work agenda. In effect, the New Deal social workers and policy wonks—often spurred by mass protest—increasingly began to call for an expansion in the prevailing understanding of rights, an expansion that supplemented the classical notion of rights with one that highlighted the importance of such positive rights as the right to a job at decent pay. For them, real freedom entailed not merely political and civil rights. That was not enough, in their minds, to guarantee the basic prerequisites of the good life. What was also needed, what was central to the fostering of real freedom, was economic rights, including the right to a job. Do away with these economic rights and you would end up with formal rather than real freedom; do away with these rights, at least according to the New Dealers, and the goal of full employment would all too easily coexist with a policy regime that allowed

5. Ibid.
6. Davidson, *Keynes Solution*, 15.

5

millions of peolpe still trapped in the quicksand of joblessness—
even in a putative full employment economy. As Harvey notes,

> In the 1940s progressives thought they could guar-
> antee the availability of enough good jobs to provide
> decent work for all job seekers, thereby moving from
> a world of perennial job shortages to one of sustained
> "full employment" in which the "right to work" would
> be secured. . . . Believing it possible to provide decent
> work for all job seekers, 1940s progressives envisioned
> a society that not only guaranteed its members the tra-
> ditional freedoms of classical liberalism, but also the
> positive rights necessary to turn formal freedom into
> real freedom, formal equality into real equality, and
> formal democracy into real democracy.[7]

The Committee on Economic Security

Actually, the progressive full-employment/right-to-work vision
can be traced back to as early as 1935. That was the year in which
the Committee on Economic Security (CES)—a cabinet level committee appointed by Roosevelt one year earlier—outlined a two-
legged approach to combat the issues of joblessness and income
assistance for the needy. The first leg, that of income assistance,
eventuated in the Social Security program and Aid to Families.
What is often forgotten is that the CES also issued a call for "employment assurance"—that is, it issued a call to develop a public
strategy and program that would meet the employment needs of
the jobless via the recognition of the federal government's duty to
promote and protect the right to work. Here's how the CES put it
in a 1935 report:

> Since most people must live by work, the first ob-
> jective in a program of economic security must be
> maximum employment. As the major contribution
> of the Federal Government in providing a safeguard

7. Harvey, "Benchmarking the Right to Work," 115.

against unemployment, we suggest employment assurance—the stimulation of private employment and the provision of public employment for those able-bodied workers whom industry cannot employ at a given time.[8]

The CES report went further: The committee called for permanent "employment assurance" since, in their view, even in "good" or "normal" economic times, large numbers of persons and communities might still be plagued by joblessness:

> Public-work programs are most necessary in times of severe depression, but may be needed in normal times, as well, to help meet the problems of stranded communities and overmanned and declining industries. To avoid the evils of hastily planned emergency work, public work should be planned in advance and coordinated with the construction and developmental policies of the Government and with the State and local public works projects.
>
> We regard work as preferable to other forms of relief where possible. While we favor unemployment compensation in cash, we believe it should be provided for limited periods . . . without government subsidies. Public funds should be devoted to providing work rather than relief.[9]

In his announcement of the creation of the CES, Roosevelt drew an explicit linkage between the committee's proposed work and the right to work itself. Referring to the general welfare and stressing the centrality of the right to work in contributing to that welfare, Roosevelt noted,

> If, as our Constitution tells us, our Federal Government was established among other things "to promote the general welfare," it is our plain duty to provide for that security upon which welfare depends. . . . The security

8. Cited in Quigley, *Ending Poverty*, 105–6.
9. Ibid., 106.

of the home, the security of livelihood, and the security
of social insurance—are, it seems to me, a minimum
. . . of the promise that we can offer to the American
people. They constitute a right which belongs to every
individual and family willing to work.[10]

The National Resources Planning Board

One finds an even more explicit link between full employment and
the right to work in a report by the National Resources Planning
Board titled "Security, Work, and Relief Policies."[11] A high-level
federal commission, the NRPB was tasked with the responsibility
of developing a comprehensive and consistent approach to ensure
that the mass unemployment that existed during the 1930s did not
rear its head again after the wind down of World War II. Totaling
over five hundred pages, its 1942 report highlights the importance
of preventing a return to the Great Depression's level of joblessness
by making a national commitment to full employment:

> The development and adoption of techniques for
> bringing about and maintaining full employment of
> men and machines is not only a major problem, but it
> is today the Nation's most pressing economic problem,
> relegating all other economic problems to a secondary
> position so long as it remains unsolved.[12]

Among the rights championed in the report are 1) "the right to
work, usefully and creatively throughout the productive years,"
and 2) "the right to fair pay, adequate to command the necessities
and amenities of life in exchange for work, ideas, thrift, and other
socially valuable services."[13]

10. Cited in Sunstein, *Second Bill of Rights*, 72.

11. For the text of the report, see http://www.ssa.gov/history/reports/
NRPB/NRPBreport.html.

12. Cited in Quigley, *Ending Poverty*, 106–7.

13. Ibid., 107.

The NRPB goes on to identify the federal government as ultimately bearing the duty of guaranteeing that jobs at "fair" or "decent" pay are available to all those who are ready, willing, and able to work. Again, what we see is the idea that if the private sector fails to provide enough jobs for all those genuinely desiring paid employment, then it becomes the responsibility of the federal government to "correct" this problem. Accordingly, the body of the proposal maintains that to "guarantee the right to a job, activities in the provision of physical facilities and services should be supplemented" by the following:

1. Formal acceptance by the Federal Government of responsibility for insuring jobs at decent pay to all those able to work regardless of whether or not they can pass a means test.

2. The preparation of plans and programs, in addition to those recommended . . . for all kinds of socially useful work other than construction, arranged according to the variety of abilities and locations of persons seeking employment.

3. Expansion of the functions of the [U.S.] Employment Service, strengthening its personnel to the end that it may operate as the key mechanism in referring unemployed workers to jobs, whether public or private.

4. Establishment of a permanent "Works Administration" under an appropriate Federal agency to administer the provision of jobs of socially desirable work for the otherwise unemployed.[14]

Importantly, the NRPB's report underscores a central aspect of the conception of full employment that took root in the thought and actions of the New Dealers—namely, that full employment has both quantitative and qualitative dimensions. For them, full employment does not simply boil down to the number of jobs; an abundance of poorly paid jobs does not constitute genuine full employment. Genuine full employment also has a qualitative dimension: not only must there be ample jobs to provide

14. Ibid.

employment to all those involuntarily unemployed, but these jobs must be "socially useful" and must pay a livable wage.

Roosevelt's Second Bill of Rights

All of the aforementioned thought found its way into Roosevelt's 1944 State of the Union address and his call for a "second Bill of Rights." Legal scholar Cass Sunstein considers this speech to be so forceful in its defense of the full-employment/right-to-work agenda that he considers it to be "the greatest of the twentieth century."[15] Whether or not one agrees with Sunstein's assessment, it is beyond doubt that Roosevelt's speech is an extraordinarily important one that posits a progressive conception of full employment as central to the building of a humane, just, and peaceful society. And here's a particularly relevant snippet from the address:

> This Republic had its beginnings, and grew to its present strength, under the protection of certain inalienable political rights—among them the right of free speech, free press, free worship, trial by jury, freedom from unreasonable searches and seizures. They were our rights to life and liberty.
>
> As our Nation has grown in size and stature, however—as our industrial economy expanded—these political rights proved inadequate to assure us equality in the pursuit of happiness.
>
> We have come to a clear realization of the fact that true individual freedom cannot exist without economic security and independence. "Necessitous men are not free men." People who are hungry and out of a job are the stuff of which dictatorships are made.
>
> In our day these economic truths have become accepted as self-evident. We have accepted, so to speak, a second Bill of Rights under which a new basis of

15. Sunstein, *Second Bill of Rights*, 1.

security and prosperity can be established for all—regardless of station, race, or creed.[16]

And, significantly, the first two items that FDR spells out in
his proposed Bill of Rights touch directly on the issue of access to
a job at an "adequate" wage, namely, "the right to a useful and remunerative job in the industries or shops or farms or mines of the
nation," and "the right to earn enough to provide adequate food
and clothing and recreation."[17]

At a more general level, then, the New Deal's public employment programs, along with the reports by the Committee on Economic Security and the National Resources Planning Board—as
well as, of course, Roosevelt's call for a second Bill of Rights—all
contributed to an expansion of public discourse about economic
rights and to the idea that, if necessary, the feds had the duty to
serve as employer of last resort—the duty, that is, to implement
and maintain an employment assurance program.

The Full Employment Act of 1945

The NRPB's report, as well as the work of the Committee on Economic Security and FDR's 1944 address, also laid the groundwork
for the Full Employment Act of 1945. Sections 2(b) and 2(c) of the
act draw a direct link between full employment, a right to work,
and, finally, the government's responsibility to assure "continuing
full employment." Section 2(b), for instance, reads as follows: "All
Americans . . . are entitled to an opportunity for useful, remunerative, regular, and full-time employment."[18] And what about Section 2(c)? Well, that's the section where it's proclaimed that the
federal government has the duty to ensure that jobs are plentiful
enough to make "useful, remunerative, regular, and full-time employment" a reality:

16. Cited in ibid., 242–43.
17. Cited in ibid., 243.
18. Cited in Santoni, "Employment Act of 1946," 8.

> In order to assure the free exercise of the right to an
> opportunity for employment . . . the Federal Govern-
> ment has the responsibility to assure continuing full
> employment, that is, the existence at all times of suf-
> ficient employment opportunities for all Americans.[19]

As part of discharging its duty, the Full Employment Act
would have required the president to submit an annual budget
to the Congress that (*a*) estimated the size of the labor force, (*b*)
gauged the level of production needed to provide jobs for that labor force, and (*c*) calculated the total investment needed to arrive
at a full-employment level of production. If the anticipated level of
production was below the level thought to be needed to provide
full employment, then the president "was required to recommend
legislation that would produce a big enough deficit to raise output
to the full employment level."[20] Now, if that's a tad bit confusing,
think of it this way: You have what you anticipate the economy
will produce in a given year and, likewise, you have an estimate of
the level of output that is needed to assure employment for those
seeking jobs. If the former is less than the latter—that is, if what is
anticipated is less than what is needed to secure full employment—
then the feds must be willing to step in and fill in the gap—which,
by the way, they can do by spending more to juice up the economy
or enacting a public jobs program. Typically, this is going to result
in an increase in the federal deficit. But you can also walk this back,
so to speak, in the opposite direction: "If the relationship between
the two output forecasts were reversed, the President was required
to recommend legislation that would result in a budget surplus big
enough to reduce output to the full employment level."[21]

Ultimately, it was a watered down version of the initial act[22]
that saw the light of day. Still, the Full Employment Act of 1945

19. Cited in ibid., 12.

20. Ibid., 9.

21. Ibid.

22. What was actually passed was the Employment Act of 1946. The
1946 Act dropped any reference to full employment and the right to work,
replacing that nomenclature with talk of "maximum" employment and the

both expanded public discourse about economic rights and represented a milestone effort to legally instantiate the full-employment/right-to-work agenda.

Losing Faith in Full Employment

If progressives of the 1930s and 1940s thought it was possible to secure full employment and the right to work, that's hardly the case today—at least according to economist Philip Harvey, one of the leading contemporary advocates of economic rights, including the right to work. According to Harvey, contemporary progressives have lost faith in the achievability of the full-employment/right-to-work agenda, and this loss of faith has resulted in progressives talking more and more about rights at work and, correspondingly, less and less about rights to work. Or, to put it another way, contemporary progressives exhibit a decided tendency to separate the qualitative and quantitative dimensions of the full-employment/right-to-work agenda. They are "strong" on such issues as working conditions, benefits, and pay at work but increasingly weak or silent on the need for public-employment schemes that ensure that everyone enjoys the right to work. Just to be clear, Harvey champions both the qualitative and quantitative dimensions of full employment. Such rights at work as pay, benefits, and workplace governance are of extreme significance. But such rights at work, says Harvey, must remain joined to the goal of creating enough jobs to ensure the right to work. Here's his take on the contemporary conundrum that characterizes progressives nowadays:

> As regards the right to work, progressives have either stopped talking about it or have sought to redefine the right in ways that de-emphasize the importance of

---

need to balance concerns about reducing joblessness with what was seen as the equally important goal of maintaining price stability—that is, being on guard against inflation. Conservative forces, in other words, were successful in defeating the attempt on the part of progressives to legally instantiate the full-employment and right-to-work agenda. For an insightful discussion, see Mucciaroni, *Political Failure*, esp. 14–44.

full employment as a means of securing it. For most progressives this has involved an increased emphasis on . . . the distributive and qualitative aspects of work (a strong commitment to equal employment opportunity and the achievement of decent wages, benefits and working conditions for all workers) and a decreased emphasis on . . . the quantitative aspect of the right to work (ensuring the availability of enough jobs to provide paid employment for everyone who wants it).[23]

A paradigmatic example of this loss of faith, according to Harvey, is the International Labour Organization's (ILO) "decent work for all" advocacy campaign. While clearly supportive of the classic rights at work, Harvey is disturbed by what he sees as the short shrift that the ILO—at least in this campaign—is giving to the right to work. What they've done, says Harvey, is to downplay, if not outright ignore, the "for all" dimension of the "decent work for all" campaign:

> When the ILO undertook to formulate an employment strategy of achieving "decent work for all," the strategy it embraced virtually ignored the quantitative aspect of the decent work vision (the "for all" part of the "decent work for all" goal) in favor of forceful advocacy of a wide range of rights at work (the "decent work" part of the goal).[24]

He continues:

> In truth, the employment strategy promoted in the ILO's *Global Employment Agenda* does not aim to achieve full employment—at least not in the 1940s sense of the term—or to secure the right to work. Fairly stated, the goal promoted in the document is merely to ensure that all paid employment is "decent" and to reduce involuntary unemployment to the minimum

23. Harvey, "Benchmarking the Right to Work," 120.
24. Ibid., 121.

level consistent with price stability while promoting increases in labor productivity to create "more room for growth oriented demand policies."[25]

Harvey fears that the ILO's stance represents a broader tendency among progressives to give up on the more robust vision that took root during the 1930s and early part of the 1940s—a vision that, to reiterate, kept rights at work and the right to work joined at hip. The loss of faith represented by the ILO, for Harvey, runs the risk of hobbling a robust and progressive vision of how we can secure full employment and realize the right to work, in both its quantitative and qualitative dimensions. And what's more, says Harvey, the right to work is so fundamental to the progressive vision of the good society that to jettison it is to jeopardize our ability to achieve a wide range of other social goods:

> The right to work occupies a particularly important position because of the role it plays in supporting efforts to secure other economic and social rights. This contributory function stems in part from the breadth of the right to work itself and in part from its effect on both the level of unmet social needs in society and the level of resources available to meet those needs. Because of this dual effect (reducing unmet needs while simultaneously increasing societal resources), a society that is successful in securing the right to work is likely to have an easy time securing the full range of economic and social rights recognized in the Universal Declaration [of Human Rights] (e.g., the right to adequate food, decent housing, adequate health care, a good education, income security for persons who are unable to be self-supporting, and so forth). On the other hand, a society that fails to secure the right to work (as most do) is likely to find it very difficult to secure other economic and social rights as well. In this respect the right to work occupies a position among economic

25. Ibid.

and social rights that is analogous to that occupied by freedom of speech among civil and political rights.[26]

But if the right to work is as fundamental as Harvey claims—if it is, in fact, "analogous to that occupied by freedom of speech among civil and political rights"—then why did progressives lose faith in its achievability? In other words, why did they stop emphasizing something on which so much else hinges, something that, according to Harvey, constitutes the very core of the progressive vision of a good society?

Explaining the Loss of Faith in the Full-Employment/ Right-to-Work Agenda

Harvey believes that the loss of faith in direct job creation as the best route to securing the full-employment/right-to-work agenda is at least partially attributable to the ascendancy of a version of Keynesian economics that emerged during and shortly after the gearing up for World War II. For this school of Keynesian economists, says Harvey, the rise of war-related employment was proof positive that the problem of joblessness could be adequately handled via macroeconomic management, that is, via a manipulation of aggregate demand:

> American progressives lost interest in the direct job-creation strategy as war-related employment—both military and civilian—finally brought the nation's lingering unemployment crisis to an end in the early 1940s. Impressed by both the ease with which war-related spending achieved this goal and the persuasiveness of John Maynard Keynes's teachings, progressives were easily convinced that the Keynesian ADM [aggregate demand management] strategy constituted both an easier and a more effective means of securing the right to work. . . . It is hardly surprising, therefore,

26. Ibid., 118.

that it was the ADM strategy rather than the direct job-creation strategy that American progressives embraced as the cornerstone of their ongoing efforts to secure the right to work following the end of World War II.[27]

In Harvey's analysis, the early 1970s, with its simultaneously high rates of joblessness and inflation, posed a serious challenge to the Keynesian ADM strategy: lowering joblessness required goosing up aggregate demand; however, increasing aggregate demand would only exacerbate inflation. Thus, being so closely associated with Keynesian ADM strategy, progressives found themselves in the conundrum of not being able to beat down unemployment without getting hammered by inflation. Particularly important, progressives had bet wrong: Their shift from a direct to an indirect approach to securing full employment was now backfiring. Blamed, even if unjustly, for the phenomenon of stagflation—and castigated for being unable to solve it—progressives found themselves on the defensive. Having cast aside the strategy of direct job creation as the best way to secure the full-employment/right-to-work agenda, and caught in the putative tradeoff between lower unemployment rates and higher inflation rates, progressives, says Harvey, have grown increasingly pessimistic about the prospects of attaining genuine full employment—ensuring decent employment for all those ready, willing, and able to work. Consequently, much of their effort is now focused on the qualitative dimension of full employment. The experience of the 1970s, in other words, has rendered them largely mute on the quantitative dimension, the dimension undergirded by a deep faith in their ability to secure the right to decent employment for all.

Harvey's thesis poses an important question for this project, namely, what in the world does this have to do with Martin Luther King, Jr.? I think an initial answer can be ventured in one word: plenty. In the next couple of chapters, I'll argue that King's theological and ethical reasoning leads him to critically retrieve the

27. Harvey, "Why Is the Right to Work So Hard to Secure?" 135.

New Dealers' full-employment/right-to-work agenda and place it at the heart of his conception of the economic prerequisites of the beloved community and his call for an economic bill of rights.

2

The Political Economy of Martin Luther King, Jr.

Theological and Ethical Underpinnings

The previous chapter demonstrates that the New Dealers popular-
ized and pursued a full-employment/right-to-work agenda. More
particularly, they advocated—and fought for—the notion that (*a*)
genuine full employment is that situation in which jobs at decent
pay are available to all those ready, willing, and able to work, (*b*)
the securing of full employment is intricately linked to the realization of the right to work, and (*c*) the feds have a duty to ensure that
all can access this right. Given their skepticism about the market's
ability to generate and sustain full employment, they tended to
believe that a strategy of direct job creation was central to securing
genuine full employment and realizing the right to work.

This strategy of direct job creation, as noted by Harvey, dif-
fers from the version of Keynesian economics that eventually
gained ascendancy among progressives and that exclusively relies
on the indirect strategy of manipulating aggregate demand to
combat joblessness. More and more economic justice advocates
have increasingly shifted their focus away from the right to work
and toward rights at work. This shift, so the story goes, reflects
a fundamental loss of faith in the full-employment/right-to-work
agenda that took root among progressives in the third and fourth
decades of the twentieth century.

You'll recall that we concluded by asking the question, what in the world does this have to do with Martin Luther King, Jr.? Or to put it in terms that are even more directly applicable to this project: What does any of this have to do with King's conception of the basic economic prerequisites of the beloved community?

To answer this question, I begin by highlighting the theological and ethical rationale that gives rise to King's response to involuntary joblessness and poverty. As we'll see, King elevates the issue of joblessness to the theological level and argues that, ultimately, it is an outright assault against the goal of community and a transgression against the norms of human dignity and inter-relatedness. Sure, involuntary joblessness and economic insecurity imposes substantial costs on both the individual and social level; but it is also important to note, at least from King's perspective, that such socioeconomic ills are an affront to the basic moral order of the universe. It is this type of reasoning that shapes King's basic political economy and ultimately leads him to issue a call for an economic bill of rights[1]—a bill that retrieves, radicalizes, and revitalizes the full-employment/right-to-work agenda that meant so much to the New Deal progressives. Before unfolding this argument, however, there's that "little" matter of what I call clatter control.

A Call to Clatter Control

Much of our public discourse about King—about his mission and message—amounts to little more than clatter, a torrent of straight-up noise and nonsense. So, if you don't know about his economic beliefs, about his views on full employment and economic rights—and about how those views are related to his conception of the beloved community—you're probably not alone. After all, it's pretty easy for one's economic arguments to get submerged when one's message has been reduced to sound bites and one's image used to sell coffee mugs, T-shirts, stamps, pajamas, underwear,

---

1. The following chapter actually takes up King's economic bill of rights.

and even thongs that promise to cover "your sweet spot without covering your assets."[2] When it comes to muffling a message, it seems that nothing beats healthy dosages of commercialization and trivialization.

This message muffling, by the way, occurs in a variety of ways. In addition to the crass commercialization associated with the pushing of assorted trinkets, King's message is muffled by what has become a national obsession with his 1963 "Dream" speech. Now, don't get me wrong: I believe that the speech, when read in its entirety and the context of the time, is both powerful and prophetic.[3] But it's undeniable that in the public's imagination this speech has been reduced to King's jazz-like riff on color and character, a reduction that tosses out with reckless abandon his references to, say, folks of color being exiled on a "lonely island of poverty" and bound by "manacles of segregation and chains of discrimination." In fact, by the nation's obsession with the "I Have a Dream Speech," by its seeming determination to freeze King at a single point in time, we've ended up with an utterly domesticated King—a King stripped of his radicalness and rendered harmless. It is this public image of King that has given rise to all sorts of clatter that references him for all sorts of causes, some of which he would have clearly opposed. Take, for instance, President Reagan, who, in 1986, seized upon King's color-and-character riff to paint King himself as an opponent of affirmative action. Here's Regan in his own words: "We are committed to a society in which all men and women have equal opportunities to succeed, and so we oppose the use of quotas. We want a colorblind society, a society that, in the words of Dr. King, judges people not on 'the color of their skin but by the content of their character.'"[4] What makes this type of clatter so stunning is that even a casual inspection of King's speeches and sermons reveals his support for programs and policies that "com-

2. See http://www.cafepress.com/+martin-luther-king-womens-thongs.

3. Hansen, *Speech that Inspired the Nation.* Hansen does an excellent job of recovering and highlighting the prophetic and radical character of King's "Dream" speech.

4. Cited in ibid., 222.

pensated" African-Americans for the harms inflicted upon them. In his 1967 testimony before the National Advisory Commission on Civil Disorders, King makes the following comments:

> The nation must not only radically readjust its attitude toward the Negro and the compelling present, but must incorporate in its planning some compensatory consideration for the handicaps he has inherited from the past. It is impossible to create a formula for the future which does not take into account that our society has been doing something special *against* the Negro for hundreds of years. How then can he be absorbed into the mainstream of American life if we do not do something special *for* him now, in order to balance the equation and equip him to compete on a just and equal basis?
>
> Whenever this issue of compensatory or preferential treatment for the Negro is raised, some of our friends recoil in horror. The Negro should be granted equality, they agree; but he should ask nothing more. On the surface, this appears reasonable, but it is not realistic. For it is obvious that if a man is entered at the starting line in a race three hundred years after another man, the first would have to perform some impossible feat in order to catch up with his fellow runner.[5]

More generally, the problem with the way in which King has been frozen in time is that it blots out his larger moral vision and, with regard to the present work, it wipes the canvass clean of his conception of the relationship between genuine full employment and the beloved community. This is, I think, the precise point Julian Bond was making when, in 1968, he lamented that the commemorations of King focused too much on "Martin Luther King the dreamer, and not on Martin Luther King the antiwar activist, not on Martin Luther King the challenger of the economic order, not on Martin Luther King the opponent of apartheid, not on the

5. Ibid., 224.

complete Martin Luther King."[6] To grasp "the complete Martin Luther King," the one who embraced and died for the full-employment/right-to-work agenda, we must ignore the clatter and, as an initial starting point, return to the vision and the moral norms that shaped his conception of the centrality of full employment to the realization of his notion of the beloved community.

King's Moral Vision: The Telos of Community

"Moral vision," write Birch and Rasmussen, "is the vision of the good we hold, a part of which is how we perceive and regard ourselves and others."[7] A moral vision, in other words, paints a picture of what we take to be the "good society," the goal toward which, we contend, our efforts ought to be directed. As such, it serves as a reference point by which we value alternative courses of action—or, as Birch and Rasmussen put it, "It confers status upon that which is of greater importance and lesser, and, indeed, of no importance at all."[8] The "good," "right," or "fitting" thing to do, then, is seen within the context of the moral vision that we embrace.

For our purposes, this raises an immediate question: What is King's moral vision? What, in other words, is King's conception of the good society, the goal toward which we ought to be striving? The short answer, not surprisingly, is this: the beloved community is the end or goal toward which all of our efforts ought to be directed. To probe deeper into the meaning of that statement, we have to peel the onion back a bit. If we do this, we'll realize that King's moral vision is translatable into the notion that the beloved community is that earthly space wherein all persons recognize their interrelatedness and seek to promote and protect human dignity.

Not clear? Well, let's get at it by beginning with how the related concepts of *imago Dei*, human dignity, and interrelatedness function in King's basic theological reasoning. For King, being

6. Ibid., 225.
7. Birch and Rasmussen, *Bible and Ethics*, 59.
8. Ibid., 62.

created in the image of God means, first of all, that each individual possesses an equal, inestimable, and inherent worth. In other words, King says, you and I have value because we are created by and related to God. Thus, in a 1962 speech before a church conference, King stated,

> Our Hebraic-Christian tradition refers to the inherent dignity of man by the biblical term the image of God. This innate worth referred to in the phrase the image of God is universally shared in equal portions by all men. There is no graded scale of essential worth, there is no divine right of one race that differs from the divine right of another. Every human being has etched in his personality the indelible stamp of the creator.[9]

Indeed, King is adamant that anything that purports to be a Christian ethic must always give pride of place to the sacredness of the human person, which, to reiterate, is derived from God's very act of creation:

> In the final analysis, says the Christian ethic, every man must be respected because God loves him. The worth of an individual does not lie in the measure of his intellect, his racial origin, or his social position. Human worth lies in relatedness to God. An individual has value because he has value to God. Whenever this is recognized, "whiteness" and "blackness" pass away as determinants in a relationship and "son" and "brother" are substituted.[10]

Take a moment and think about King's words and you'll see that, for King, *imago Dei*, human worth, and relatedness are inextricably linked: Persons have intrinsic worth because they are created by and related to God, and, furthermore, being created by God means that persons are related to each other. In other words, King's theological and ethical reasoning is expressive of what Peter

9. King, "The Ethical Demands for Integration," in Washington, *Testament of Hope*, 118–19.

10. Ibid., 122.

Paris calls the principle of the parenthood of God and the kinship of all peoples. On this point, Paris offers the following observation:

> King believed strongly in the idea that all people are related to each other, because God is the parent of all. Further, it was his view that community with one another and God was the end for which its creator intended humanity.[11]

What's more, King understands the theological principle of the parenthood of God and the kinship of all peoples as proof that (*a*) God works within history to restore community, and (*b*) one cannot harm community without doing serious harm to oneself and others. God, says King, creates humans for communion with one another and with God. In short, community is the end for which humanity is created. The interrelatedness so characteristic of community is such an embedded part of God's moral order that it is straight up impossible for you or me to become fully ourselves outside of concern and love for each other. In fact, for King, this concern and love for each other—this acknowledgment of inter-relatedness and respect for human dignity—constitutes the "first law of life":

> From time immemorial men have lived by the principle that "self-preservation is the first law of life." But this is a false assumption. I would say that other-preservation is the first law of life. It is the first law of life precisely because we cannot preserve self without being concerned about preserving other selves. The universe is so structured that things go awry if men are not diligent in their cultivation of the other-regarding dimension. "I" cannot reach fulfillment without "thou." The self cannot be self without other selves.[12]

---

11. Paris, *Black Religious Leaders*, 112.
12. King, *Where Do We Go from Here?*, 210.

Human Dignity, Community,
and Interrelatedness as Moral Norms

Community, human dignity, and interrelatedness also function as basic moral norms, as reference points, so to speak, by which we ought to evaluate our individual and collective actions. Norms, as Hak Joon Lee observes, "serve as the standards to assess civil laws, government policies, and social mores and practices, and a common moral ground in rallying people for a social cause."[13] For King, the basic issue boils down to this: Do our actions contribute to the formation or the destruction of community? Are we pursing social, economic, and political policies that promote and respect human dignity? Or are we walking—or perhaps running—down a path that disregards interrelatedness and results in socioeconomic marginalization? If, as King contends, community is the end for which God creates us, then by engaging in anti-community actions, we not only violate the Divine will but we also degrade the quality of our lives together. Again, Paris is instructive on this point:

> It follows, therefore, that those who act for the destruc-
> tion of such community not only violate God's will
> but become involved in their own self-destruction as
> well. In other words, since we are all kinspeople, the
> degree to which I harm that relationship in any way
> I harm myself. My personhood is integrally related to
> the kinship of all. Thus, the agent of the harm as well
> as the one harmed are victimized and are in need of
> liberation. This line of thought led King to espouse an
> important principle: Those who work for community
> must resist those who work against it. . . . Since God
> works in the world to restore broken community, God's
> followers can do no other.[14]

And here's something to note, something that can be easily overlooked: In King's theological and ethical reasoning, the "good

13. Lee, *Great World House*, 122.
14. Paris, *Black Religious Leaders*, 112.

person" is the one whose actions contribute to the actualization of the beloved community. Or to look at it from another vantage point, the "good person" recognizes that we are all inescapably dependent upon each other and, therefore, embedded in a vast network of interrelatedness—and she acts accordingly. As moral agents, then, we are tasked with the responsibility of cooperating with the Divine to restore community.

More generally, King consistently contends that, as individuals, we need to envision ourselves as persons-in-community rather than as isolated nomads who are solely responsible for our fates. And, as persons-in-community, one of the ways in which we faithfully discharge our responsibilities is by demanding and fighting for a polis that allows no one to languish in economic idleness—a community, that is, that ensures that each and every one of us is protected against the potential ravages of economic insecurity.

A Kingian Explanation of Economic Insecurity

King's vision of the beloved community—as well as the associated norms of community, human dignity, and interrelatedness—exerts a powerful impact on his proposed ethical actions for combating two of the primary forms of economic insecurity, namely, the twin problems of joblessness and poverty. Before delving into this relationship, however, it will prove useful to briefly probe what King sees as the fundamental causes of economic security.

Looking toward the horizon, King sees, first of all, an economic tsunami that, if left unchecked, threatens to exacerbate existing joblessness and further destabilize the economic foundations that are absolutely essential to a healthy community. More particularly, it is the uncontrolled whirlwinds of automation, deindustrialization, and economic restructuring that threaten to put millions of people in dire straits. In a 1961 speech before the United Automobile Workers (UAW), King made the following remarks:

The automobile industry is not alone a production complex of assembly lines and steel-forming equipment. It is an industry of people who must live in decency with the security for children, for old age, for health and cultural life. Automation cannot be permitted to become a blind monster which grinds out more cars and simultaneously snuffs out the hopes and lives of the people by whom the industry was built.[15]

Four years later, in a speech before the Illinois AFL-CIO, King made the same point, warning labor of the nasty impact of economic restructuring on regions such as Appalachia. In the absence of a proactive response, economic restructuring will wreak havoc on labor's bargaining strength, according to King:

Unfortunately, labor cannot stand still long or it will slip backward. Apart from its loss of influence and leadership, the new technology is undermining its strength. The advance of automation is a destructive hurricane whose winds are sweeping away jobs and work standards. . . .

One of the most publicized areas of the poor, Appalachia, is the huge ghost town of the mining industry overcome by automation and new products. In a few years, steel will have lost one-third of the jobs it had in 1950 as new methods and equipment blot out employment. Food packing, auto and electrical assembly, all industries of this state, are visibly scarred by the consuming flames of automation. The process does not abate because it has socially undesirable consequences, but accelerates because it is invariably profitable to industry to shrink jobs.[16]

But King's views are not limited to empirical observations about the impact of technological changes on the level of

15. Speech to the United Automobile Workers Union, Detroit, Michigan, April 27, 1961, cited in Honey, *"All Labor Has Dignity"*, 27.

16. Speech to the Illinois AFL-CIO, Springfield, Illinois, October 7, 1965, cited in Honey, *"All Labor Has Dignity"*, 115.

joblessness. He also contends that the historical record provides ample evidence that American capitalism is plagued by a chronic jobs gap, a persistent chasm between the number of jobs available and the numbers of persons in need of employment. In his view, then, the job gap is present even in economic good times—that is, the mismatch between the number of jobs available and the numbers of person desiring employment is present even at the top of the business cycle. To put it mildly, King is skeptical of any claim that the logic of the market can eliminate unemployment, underemployment, and poverty, and thereby ensure that all can enjoy basic economic security:

> We've come a long way in our understanding . . . of the blind operation of our economic system. Now we realize that dislocations in the market operation of our economy and the prevalence of discrimination thrust people into idleness and bind them in constant or frequent unemployment against their will. . . . We also know that no matter how dynamically the economy develops and expands, it does not eliminate poverty.[17]

Racial Discrimination and Economic Restructuring: A Deadly Brew

For King, economic restructuring, the outsourcing of jobs, and free-market logic interacts with the dynamics of racial discrimination to generate heightened levels of joblessness among people and communities of color. Given the rather "warm and fuzzy" images of him that often circulate in the popular media and public discourse, it's easy to forget that King never pulled his punches when it came to decrying the injustice of racial domination. King thought it was utter nonsense to claim that African-Americans were disproportionately poor and jobless because they were a bunch of malingerers, always on the lookout for ways to avoid work and responsibility.

17. King, *Where Do We Go from Here?*, 191.

When he looked at the economic plight of communities of color, communities ravaged by astronomical levels of joblessness and poverty, he never saw them as places seething with immorality and moral deficiencies. What he saw were a people who, because of the historical legacy of discrimination, had been denied the opportunity to build levels of human and social capital that could at least serve as a partial buffer against the threat of economic misery—a people who, because of massive discrimination in both the public and private sectors, found themselves situated in the very jobs that were most vulnerable to the economic winds of technological change and the outsourcing of jobs. Consider, for instance, these words delivered in a 1962 speech before the United Packinghouse Workers of America:

> Negroes are already deeply affected by the unemployment engendered by automation. Long years of deprivation of opportunity have robbed us of the skills needed to utilize new industrial devices. Thus, even before we have achieved elementary human rights, many of us are threatened by catastrophic economic disabilities.[18]

King leaves no doubt that, in his mind, racial discrimination contributes mightily to the massive jobs crisis that afflicts African-Americans—an affliction, again, that is made worse by the economic turbulence of automation and runaway jobs. African-Americans, says King, are being left further and further behind:

> It is a bitter and ironic truth that in today's prosperity, millions of Negroes live in conditions identical with or worse than the Depression thirties. For hundreds of thousands there is no unemployment insurance, no social security, no Medicare, no minimum wage. The laws do not cover their form of employment. For millions of others, there is no employment or underemployment.

18. Speech to the United Packinghouse Workers Union of America, Minneapolis, Minnesota, May 21, 1962, cited in Honey, "*All Labor Has Dignity*", 52.

In some ghettos, the present rate of unemployment is higher than that of the thirties. Education for our children is second class, and in the higher levels, so limited it has no significance as a lever for uplift. The tenements we inhabited thirty years ago, which were old then, are three decades more dilapidated. Discrimination still smothers initiative and humiliates the daily life of young and old. The progress of the nation has not carried the Negro with it; it has favored a few and bypassed the millions.[19]

All of this—the massive jobs crisis afflicting ordinary workers, the wreckage left behind in the wake of a restructuring economy and runaway shops, and the elevated levels of African-American joblessness due to racial discrimination and diminishing economic opportunities—leads King to conclude that the nation is "sick" and overflowing with "trouble in the land."[20] And nowhere is this moral sickness and trouble more evident, says King, than in what he considers to be gross violations of the norms of human dignity, community, and interrelatedness.

Economic Murder and Strangulation: Economic Insecurity as an All-Out Assault on Human Dignity, Community, and Interrelatedness

According to King, joblessness—and the impoverishment that often accompanies it—is nothing less than an all-out assault on the norms of community, human dignity, and interrelatedness. Think about this, says King: what "message" do we send to our brothers and sisters when we seem more than willing to tolerate millions of persons languishing in joblessness? What we tell them, and what we tell ourselves, is that they don't matter—that in our eyes they are nobodies. And this message, as King well knows, is particularly

19. Speech to the Illinois AFL-CIO, Springfield, Illinois, October 7, 1965, cited in Honey, *"All Labor Has Dignity"*, 117–18.

20. King, "Promised Land," in Washington, *Testament of Hope*, 280.

demoralizing in a society such as ours "whose measure of value revolves about money":

> But dignity is corroded by poverty no matter how poetically we invest the humble with simple graces and charm. No worker can maintain his morale or sustain his spirit if in the market place his capacities are declared to be worthless to society. . . . [I]n his search for human dignity he is handicapped by the stigma of poverty in a society whose measure of value revolves about money.[21]

This erosion of dignity and self-esteem is so serious that King likens its effects to "psychological murder" and economic "strangulation." On this view, economic insecurity places a chokehold on its victims and thereby deprives them of the requisite resources to meet their basic needs and to meaningfully participate in the broader community:

> In our society it is murder, psychologically, to deprive a man of a job or income. You are in substance saying to that man that he has no right to exist. You are in a real way depriving him of life, liberty, and the pursuit of happiness, denying in his case the very creed of society. Now, millions of people are being strangled in that way.[22]

And if "murder" and "strangulation" aren't alarming enough, then consider the fact that on other occasions King likens economic insecurity to a "cancerous cell" that, left untreated, metastasizes and weakens both the individual and the body politic. In a 1961 speech to the AFL-CIO, for instance, he observes, "Hardcore unemployment is now an ugly and unavoidable fact of life. Like malignant cancer, it has grown year by year and continues its spread."[23]

21. King, *Where Do We Go from Here?*, 102.

22. King, "The Trumpet of Conscience," in Washington, *Testament of Hope*, 648.

23. Speech to the AFL-CIO Fourth Constitutional Convention, Miami

King reasons that as a "malignant cancer," joblessness and poverty have a deleterious effect on community. There are social costs associated with economic insecurity, namely, high crime rates, drug abuse, domestic violence, teen pregnancy, and gang warfare, not to mention basic mistrust. We delude ourselves, King tells us, if we believe that joblessness and poverty impose a cost only on the unemployed or impoverished. When we violate the moral norms of community, human dignity, and interrelatedness, we all ultimately suffer. To reiterate, King is convinced that economic insecurity is one of the factors that contribute to our widely acknowledged social problems:

> There is always the understandable temptation to seek negative and self-destructive solutions [to economic insecurity]. Some seek a passive way out by yielding to the feeling of inferiority; or by allowing the floodgates of defeat to open with an avalanche of despair; or by dropping out of high school; or by turning to the escape valves of narcotics and alcohol. Others seek a defiant way out. Through antisocial behavior, overt delinquency and gang warfare, they release their pent-up vindictiveness on the whole society. They trust no one and do not expect others to trust them. Meanness becomes their dominating characteristic. Still others seek to deal with the dilemma through the path of isolation. They have the fantasy of a separate black nation within the nation. This approach is the most cynical and nihilistic of all, because it is based on a loss of faith in the possibilities of American democracy.[24]

Now, let's be clear here. King is not engaging in some blame-the-victim politics. The social ills that he speaks of are the direct results of our failure to combat the anti-community forces of economic insecurity. While such dysfunctional behaviors as dropping out of school and gang warfare certainly compound the problems of the economically maimed, they are not—at least in

Beach, Florida, December 11, 1961, in Honey, "All Labor Has Dignity", 39.

24. King, *Where Do We Go from Here?*, 144.

King's eyes—the cause of joblessness and poverty. For him, then, the direction of causation runs from economic insecurity to dysfunctional behavior and social ills, not the other way around. His reasoning, then, implies that the most efficacious and just route to eliminating these social ills lies in the realization of a beloved community, a community that views joblessness and poverty as a blight on human dignity and, therefore, assigns the highest of priorities to the complete eradication of economic insecurity.

In general, then, King understands joblessness and poverty to be corrosive of community, human dignity, and interrelatedness. The challenge, therefore, is to establish social and political arrangements that are commensurate with the sacredness of the person and responsive to the Divine call to community. For King this means, at the very least, the establishment of socioeconomic arrangements that respect and promote civil, political, and economic rights, with this last including, as I show in the next section, the right to a job at a livable wage—or, which amounts to the same thing, the realization of genuine full employment. Accordingly, toward the end of his life King issued a call for "an economic bill or rights to supplement the Constitution's political bill of rights."[25] In effect, he retrieves and revitalizes the conception of full employment that took root among progressives during the New Deal era and places it at the center of his conception of the beloved community. It is, then, to this "economic bill of rights"—and its relationship to the beloved community—that I now direct my attention.

25. Ibid., 231–32.

3

Full Employment, Right to Work, and the Beloved Community

The Structure and Fundamental Principles of King's Economic Bill of Rights

So, as we have seen, King contends that a socioeconomic arrangement that tolerates joblessness and poverty is in violation of the moral norms of community, human dignity, and interrelatedness. In his judgment, such economic ills pull us away from the realization of the beloved community, affront the very notion of human dignity, and place us in opposition to Divine justice. When we countenance joblessness and poverty, when we tolerate millions of our sisters and brothers languishing in economic misery, we are defying the very moral laws by which God has structured the cosmos.

Yet, King is acutely aware that condemnation is not enough; we must draw upon and then go beyond our moral outrage at a policy regime that seems all too willing to allow millions to be cast aside as human scrap, a regime that is all too willing to make a troubling peace with economic misery. We must, says King, advance and struggle for policies that move us toward the realization of the beloved community. For King this meant, among other things, retrieving and revitalizing the full-employment/right-to-work-agenda that gripped the imagination of so many progressives during the 1930s and 1940s. What is needed, urges King, is nothing less than an economic bill of rights that promotes and protects human dignity, recognizes our interrelatedness, and contributes to the restoration of community.

King as a Champion of the Right to Work

King's writings, sermons, and speeches are replete with reflections on the social and economic implications of his underlying theological reasoning and moral vision. Nowhere is this clearer, perhaps, than in the link that he makes between human dignity and human rights. For King, humans have rights *qua* humans because they are created by God and, therefore, possess inestimable worth. Each and every one of us, proclaims King, "is heir to a legacy of dignity and worth" and thus has "certain basic rights that are neither conferred by nor derived from the state . . . for they are God-given."[1] Of particular concern to us, these "God-given" rights are not confined to the classical civil and political rights; they also include economic rights. So, Hak Joon Lee is on point when he observes that

> King's commitment to human dignity led him to uphold economic rights as an integral aspect of human rights, which went beyond the boundary of the U.S. Constitution. He declared, "I have the audacity to believe that people everywhere can have three meals a day for their bodies, education and culture for their minds, and dignity, equality, and freedom for their spirits."[2]

While the securing of civil and political rights is obviously of supreme importance, King's theological and ethical reasoning also drove him to an appreciation of the centrality of economic rights in protecting human dignity and in restoring community. He was convinced that, in the absence of the right to basic economic goods, people would find it difficult to fully enjoy their civil and political

1. King, *Where Do We Go from Here?*, 98.
2. Lee, *Great World House*, 56.

rights. True protection of human dignity, then, was predicated on the interdependency of civil, political, and economic rights. Thus, for instance, King contends that a right to a job and housing are as morally absolute as, say, the right to vote: "It's not a constitutional right that men have jobs, but it is a human right."[3] King is adamant that people possess economic rights, even if those rights are not embedded in the Constitution:

> Now we are approaching areas where the voice of the Constitution is not clear. We have left the realm of constitutional rights and we are entering the realm of human rights.
>
> The Constitution assured the right to vote, but there is no such assurance of the right to adequate housing, or the right to an adequate income. And yet, in a nation which has a gross domestic product of 750 billion dollars a year, it is morally right to insist that every person has a decent house, an adequate education and enough money to provide basic necessities for one's family.[4]

To reiterate, in King's mind the protection and promotion of human dignity—as well as the restoration of community—hinges upon the interdependency of civil, political, and economic rights. If economic rights, including the right to a job, are missing from the picture, King contends, we merely "exist." Human flourishing is simply not possible unless, in addition to the classical civil and political rights, we also secure rights of an economic nature. Accordingly, in a sermon delivered on March 31, 1968—just days before his assassination—he states,

> We read one day—We hold these truths to be self-evident, that all men are created equal, that they are endowed by their creator with certain inalienable rights. That among these are life, liberty and the pursuit of happiness. But if a man doesn't have a job or an income,

3. Jackson, *From Civil Rights to Human Rights*, 244.
4. King, *Where Do We Go from Here?*, 153.

he has neither life nor liberty nor the possibility for the pursuit of happiness. He merely exists.[5]

What do we need in order to move beyond "mere existence"? King's answer could hardly be more direct: we need an economic floor beneath which no one is allowed to sink; we need economic pillars that enable all persons to flourish and live a life of dignity within the context of community; we need jobs for the jobless and income support for those who are not able or not expected to participate in the paid labor market. In short, we need the instantiation of an "economic bill of rights to supplement the Constitution's political Bill of Rights."[6] For King, this supplementation of the political with an economic bill of rights is central to the broadening of democracy and part of the requisite foundational underpinnings of a blessed community that respects and promotes human dignity. And, as I argue in the next section, the progressive full-employment/right-to-work agenda resides at the very heart of King's proposed economic bill of rights.

Full Employment as the Centerpiece of King's Economic Bill of Rights

King contended, especially during the last three years of his life, that we had it within our power to secure genuine full employment and realize the right to work. A just society, he proclaims, guarantees jobs at livable wages to all who are ready, willing, and able to work but who haven't secured employment in the private sector. In his 1966 testimony before the Senate Subcommittee on Urban Reorganization, for instance, he maintains that the government is morally bound to eliminate joblessness and poverty through a policy regime of guaranteed jobs and guaranteed income: "If the society changes its concepts by placing the responsibility on its

---

5. King, "Remaining Awake Through a Great Revolution," in Washington, *Testament of Hope*, 274.

6. King, *Where Do We Go from Here?*, 232.

system, not on the individual, and guarantees secure employment or guaranteed income, dignity will come within the reach of all."[7]

By the way, when King calls for "placing responsibility on the system, not on the individual," he is not making a case for individual irresponsibility. You have to remember that, for King, joblessness and poverty primarily result from the logic of free-market capitalism, structural changes in the economy, runaway shops, declines in the demand for unskilled labor, and straight-up racial discrimination. These problems are so pervasive as to be systemic, and their resolution is beyond the "self-help" activities of the economically insecure. Persons must and should do all that they can to raise their heads above the choppy waters of joblessness and poverty, but in the final analysis, says King, it is simply unrealistic to expect individuals to shoulder the enormous burden of eradicating poverty and joblessness. As King puts it,

> While there must be continued emphasis on the need for blacks to pool their economic resources and withdraw consumer support from discriminating firms, we must not be oblivious to the fact that the larger economic problems confronting the Negro community will only be solved by federal programs involving billions of dollars.[8]

Thus, while he never rejects the idea that the economically deprived have a moral responsibility to pool their resources to support entrepreneurship and to develop habits of thrift, he holds firm to the conviction that the "ultimate" answer to the problem of economic insecurity "will be found in a massive federal program for all the poor along the lines of A. Philip Randolph's Freedom Budget, a kind of Marshall Plan for the disadvantaged."[9]

In any case, King's allusion to Randolph's Freedom Budget is instructive for apprehending his conception of full employment and its centrality to his own call for an economic bill of rights.

7. Long, *Against Us, but For Us*, 188.
8. King, *Where Do We Go from Here?*, 57.
9. Ibid., 244.

The underlying principle behind the Freedom Budget, proposed by Randolph in 1965, is that it is "economically feasible for the federal government to accept the responsibility for full employment, and that it was the duty of the government to take care of its people when they were unable to take care of themselves."[10] More specifically, Randolph's Freedom Budget proposed a job guarantee for all those ready, willing, and able to work, a guaranteed income for those unable to work and those who should not be working, and a living wage to lift the working poor out of poverty. Randolph thought that a national expenditure of $18.5 billion over a ten-year period would more than cover the cost of implementing such a full-employment/right-to-work agenda, with due concern, again, paid to those who either could not or were not expected to participate in the paid labor force.

These ideas extend at least as far back to the New Deal era, and King wastes no time in incorporating them into his own call for an economic bill of rights. In particular, King's proposed economic bill of rights revolves around the twin principles of an employment guarantee and an income guarantee. The first principle, the employment guarantee, upholds the right of all persons to a job paying a livable or decent wage. In King's thought, this principle is the functional equivalent of genuine full employment, with the federal government bearing the ultimate responsibility for insuring that this right is realized. The second principle, that of a guaranteed income, functions to assure that even those who are unable to participate in the paid labor force can still have access to a standard of living commensurate with human dignity.

King, I believe, views these two principles as complementary rather than mutually exclusive. The first priority is full employment, that is, guaranteeing—as a human right—that all able-bodied persons are able secure decent employment. And you'll notice, by the way, that his conception of full employment includes both the *right to work* and *rights at work*. In a 1967 televised news interview, he cast this complementarity this way:

10. Pfeffer, *A. Philip Randolph*, 288.

> Let me say this: that I am not guaranteeing—I mean calling for a guaranteed annual wage as a substitute for a guaranteed job. I think that ought to be the first thing, that we guarantee every person capable of working a job. There are many things that we need to be done that could be done that's not being done now. And this could provide the jobs.[11]

He continues to clarify this complementary relationship when he says,

> I'm speaking of a guaranteed annual wage as minimum income for every American family, so that there is an economic floor, and nobody falls beneath that. And of course, there are definitely going to be people all along, people who are unemployable, as a result of age, as a result of lack of something that failed to develop here or there, and as a result of physical disability. Now these are the people who just couldn't work. Certainly they have a right to have an income. If one has a right to life, liberty and the pursuit of happiness, then he has a right to have an income.[12]

Finally, there's this:

> I feel first that we ought to talk about guaranteed jobs; then the guaranteed annual income would be the minimum wage, which ought to be beyond the poverty level, that everyone would get in this country.[13]

But in King's economic bill of rights, jobs are also "first" in another sense: He rails against any and all attempts to emphasize "training" over the securing of the full-employment/right-to-work agenda. What's the problem with prioritizing training over job assurance?

---

11. King, "Face to Face," in Washington, *Testament of Hope*, 394.
12. Ibid.
13. Ibid.

The problem, first of all, is that this approach assumes that there is something "wrong" or "defective" in the economically marginalized that must be corrected. This approach zeroes in on the "supply side" and assumes that the problem of joblessness and poverty is best addressed by improving the weak skill sets that the poor allegedly possess and instilling in them the "right" attitudes and values central to labor market success. While King is obviously not against the provision of training to the jobless, you're on a bridge to nowhere, he says, when you overlook the chronic job gap that is characteristic of free market capitalism—which, again, is compounded by the forces of automation and the movement of jobs to low-wage regions, both in the United States and overseas. In such situations, in which the norm is typically a lack of decent-paying jobs, providing training alone is highly unlikely to significantly reduce the economic misery of the jobless and impoverished. In fact, when jobs at livable wages are scarce, putting an emphasis on "training" is like being dressed up with no place to go. If you're involuntarily unemployed, if you're swimming against the tides of joblessness and impoverishment, you have an immediate need for secure employment. While being "dressed up" is nice and should never be underestimated, the fact of the matter remains that the "well-dressed" jobless need somewhere to "go." So, for King, the guiding principle is this: "Jobs first, training later."[14]

So, for King, a strategy of direct job creation enables us to secure full employment and to realize the right to work. And this, as we've seen, requires that the jobless have someplace "to go"—requires, in other words, the provision of an ample supply of decent-paying jobs so that no able-bodied person who desires to work instead languishes in idleness. We've also seen that King is convinced that the resolution of joblessness and poverty is beyond the powers of individuals acting alone. Given the massive scope of the problem, it will take the full weight of the federal government, says King, to insure the right to work and thereby secure genuine full employment. The flip side of rights, as he well knew, is correlative duties. Someone or something must be duty-bound

14. King, *Where Do We Go from Here?*, 229.

to insure that persons are able to genuinely access and enjoy their rights. With specific reference to the securing of genuine full employment, King contends that the government is morally bound to serve as employer of last resort. While much of this has been implied in the foregoing, we are now in a position to undertake a more explicit treatment of this issue.

Divine Justice and Atonement: The State as Employer of Last Resort

King offers at least two reasons why the state bears the responsibility for assuring jobs at decent pay by acting as an employer of last resort; one is practical, the other is theological. We've already encountered the practical reason: it simply makes no sense to expect individuals to overcome the variety of forces that King believes underlies the problem of joblessness and poverty. Individuals are relatively powerless in the face of an economic restructuring process that leads to joblessness. Acting alone, they cannot put a stop to runaway shops or root out, once and for all, every vestige of racial discrimination. The economically marginalized cannot bear these kinds of burdens, and King thinks it would be downright cruel to say to them, "You all are on your own." So, again, it is impractical to expect the millions of persons mired in joblessness and poverty to dig themselves out of the economic quagmire.

But the issue is not only, or even primarily, of a pragmatic nature. That is, King avers that the state is under a divine mandate to pursue justice and, therefore, his normative view of the state is that it is morally obligated to establish the material conditions that underpin the beloved community. The state is to be judged, then, by the extent to which its activities and policies are congruent with the divine mandate to respect the sacredness of the person, to acknowledge interrelatedness, and to work for the restoration of community. In fact, this is a consistent theme throughout King's writings, sermons, and speeches. Take, for instance, his "Letter from Birmingham Jail" (1963), in which he makes it clear that state policies are subject to a higher law:

A just law is a man-made law that squares with the moral law or the law of God. An unjust law is a code that is out of harmony with the moral law . . . not rooted in eternal law and natural law. Any law that uplifts human personality is just. Any law that degrades human personality is unjust. All segregation statutes are unjust because segregation distorts the soul and damages the personality. It gives the segregator a false sense of superiority, and the segregated a false sense of inferiority. . . . So segregation is not only politically, economically, and socially unsound, but it is morally wrong and sinful.[15]

Or—to cite another example—how about that March 18, 1968, speech delivered in Memphis, Tennessee? That's the one in which he proclaimed that America was in danger of going straight to hell—that is, unless the nation reversed course and pursued economic justice. After spending a considerable part of the speech talking about the issues of job loss, unemployment, low wages, and underemployment, King utters these words:

And I come by here to say that America . . . is going to hell if she doesn't use her wealth. If America does not use her vast resources of wealth to end poverty and make it possible for all of God's children to have the basic necessities of life, she, too, will go to hell. And I will hear America through her historians, years and generations to come, saying, "We built gigantic buildings to kiss the skies. We built gargantuan bridges to span the seas. Through our spaceships we were able to carve highways through the stratosphere. Through our airplanes we were able to dwarf distance and place time in chains. Through our submarines we were able to penetrate oceanic depths."[16]

15. King, "Letter from Birmingham Jail," in Washington, *Testament of Hope*, 293.

16. Speech to AFSCME, Memphis, Tennessee, March 18, 1968, cited in Honey, *"All Labor Has Dignity,"* 173–74.

But ultimately, says King, nations are not judged by their buildings, bridges, spaceships, and submarines. They are judged by the extent to which their policies aid in wiping out joblessness and poverty and moving us closer to the realization of the beloved community. They are judged, in short, by whether they faithfully reflect the mandates of Divine justice:

> It seems that I can hear the God of the universe saying, "Even though you have done all that, I was hungry and you fed me not, I was naked and you clothed me not. The children of my sons and daughters were in need of economic security and you did not provide it for them. And so you cannot enter the kingdom of greatness." This may well be the indictment on America. And that same voice says in Memphis to the mayor, to the power structure, "If you do it unto the least of these of my children you do it unto me."[17]

What we see here, then, is that King understands Divine justice to be acutely concerned with meeting the needs of the economically marginalized. By extension, the good or just state is the one that mirrors such justice; it is the state that takes steps to tend to the needs of "the least of these." And one way in which the state can do this is by implementing an economic bill of rights, which would reduce joblessness and poverty by making the state an employer of last resort—guaranteeing jobs to all those involuntarily unemployed and guaranteeing income to all those not able or not expected to work.

On other occasions King also suggested that by implementing an economic bill of rights and acting as an employer of last resort, the state could begin the much-needed process of atoning for its sins of racism and economic exploitation. In particular, he saw the economic marginalization of black folk as the sour fruit of centuries of racial subordination. "Few people," he argued, "consider the fact that, in addition to being enslaved for two centuries, the Negro

17. Ibid., 174.

was, during all those years, robbed of the wages of his toil."[18] As Long observes, "King believed that 'no amount of gold could provide adequate compensation'" for the centuries of economic harm inflicted on African-Americans.[19] Accordingly, he believed that by acting as an employer of last resort, by guaranteeing genuine full employment and income to the economically marginalized, the state could atone for its sins by enacting a policy that would begin the process of repaying the debt owed to black labor.

All of the foregoing drives home, I think, yet another point: King clearly diverges from those who contend that the sole purpose of the state is to maintain law and order. As Michael G. Long notes, there is very little, if anything, in the corpus of King's work to suggest that he saw maintaining order as the only role of the state, and, as Long explains, King certainly disagreed with Martin Luther's view of the origins of the state:

> Interestingly, King separated himself, on the issue of the origin of the state, from Martin Luther, who had located the origin in the fall of humanity from a life of perfect grace and in divine need to rectify that fall. Luther held that the state arose because wicked people, especially non-Christians, would otherwise murder one another and plunge the world into chaos where no one could serve God. There is nothing in King's writings to suggest that he intentionally tried to be at odds with Luther on the subject of the origin of the state, but his separation from Luther allowed him to refrain from stressing only the coercive dimension of the state.[20]

Long goes on to argue, quite persuasively, that King's writings suggest that he "understood the state as an institution that has its roots in the natural inclination of the human person to depend upon and relate to others."[21] Because he believes that we

18. Cited in Long, *Against Us, but For Us,* 133.
19. Ibid.
20. Ibid., 122.
21. Ibid., 121.

are created for community, King insists that the state also has a direct and positive role to play in the creation of the beloved community. The state, then, must do more than keep us in check so that we don't tear each other's eyeballs out. Its primary duty, King implies, is to enhance the quality of our lives together. And, again, the state can accomplish this enhancement by establishing the basic preconditions for the beloved community—including, as I have stressed above, the basic economic prerequisite of genuine full employment.

The Issue of Fiscal Feasibility: Can We Afford It?

A number of criticisms, both friendly and hostile, could potentially be leveled at King's call for the government to serve as an employer of last resort. To cover all the potential critiques is beyond the scope of this text. There is one, however, that demands immediate attention: that the full-employment/right-to-work agenda is simply unaffordable and that any effort to realize it would only increase the nation's debt and spike an inflationary spiral. King's proposal, so the argument goes, sounds like a straight-up budget buster that will only prove that the road to hell is paved with good intentions. It might sound good, but the price of the ticket is way too high.

Or is it? Is it really beyond our means? Is our collective pocketbook really too thin and tattered to seriously consider such an approach to the eradication of joblessness and poverty? I don't think so; I believe that King's full-employment/right-to-work agenda is indeed fiscally feasible. It can be done! In fact, in the next two chapters I'll try to convince you of the fiscal feasibility of the approach advocated by King, and I'll do so by bringing his voice into conversation with a couple of contemporary economists who are advocating an approach to the eradication of joblessness and poverty that bears a remarkable resemblance to that advocated by King. And, as I've already alluded to above, these contemporary voices offer what I believe are compelling reasons for rejecting the fiscal infeasibility argument. These contemporary voices, then, can serve as an invaluable resource for those who, like King, are convinced that genuine full employment is absolutely central to the eradication of joblessness and the realization of the beloved community.

4

The Contribution of William A. Darity, Jr.

A National Investment Employment Corps

Moral outrage against joblessness and poverty does not begin with King's call for an economic bill of rights, of course. Neither does it end with his 1968 assassination. King is, in fact, part of a noble tradition of scholars, activists, and policymakers who have long championed economic rights, who have long envisioned a polis in which involuntary joblessness and poverty would finally be abolished—a polis in which personal and social development would no longer be stunted by economic marginalization. And, as we saw in the previous chapters, King considered the realization of the full-employment/right-to-work agenda to be absolutely essential to the conception of the beloved community.

This chapter describes a recent proposal for the eradication of involuntary joblessness made by William A. Darity, Jr. A well-known and respected scholar, Darity is currently Arts and Sciences Professor of Public Policy and Professor of African and African-American Studies and Economics at Duke University. A recipient of a PhD in economics from the Massachusetts Institute of Technology, Darity's areas of expertise are stratification economics, racial and ethnic economic inequality, and financial crises in developing countries. He is also a past president of the National Economics Association and the Southern Economics Association. But, as I've already indicated, what is of particular importance for us is how he proposes to secure full employment and realize the right to work. His proposal, which calls for the establishment of a National Investment Employment Corps, amounts to a functional equivalent of King's call for an economic bill of rights.

In the remainder of this chapter, I'll describe the basic structure of Darity's proposal, paying particular attention to the underlying sources of his vision, as well as the benefits and costs that he estimates would be attached to his National Investment Employment Corps. Before doing so, however, it's worthwhile to pause and take note of what both Darity and Harvey deem to be the personal and social costs that joblessness imposes.

The Personal and Social Costs of Joblessness and Poverty

Joblessness is no joke: It does damage both to the jobless individual and to the broader society. On the personal level, lose your job and you very well may lose your sleep, your relationships, your health, your home, and even your mind. Research consistently finds the following:[1]

- Joblessness is dangerous to your personal health: compared to persons who are continuously employed, those who lose a job through no fault of their own are more likely to develop health-related problems.

- Joblessness causes stress and leads to alterations in health behavior: lose your job and you may end up smoking more, eating more, and exercising less. There's also a good chance that you'll end up drinking more.

- Joblessness destabilizes relationships and erodes self-esteem: compared to the continuously employed, jobless persons are more likely to avoid social encounters with family and friends, contributing to strained relationships and an erosion of self-esteem.

1. See Peck, *Pinched*, 19–21.

Journalist Don Peck describes how one economist, Andrew Oswald, avers that joblessness undermines personal happiness:

> According to Andrew Oswald, an economist at the University of Warwick, in the United Kingdom, and a pioneer in the field of happiness studies, no other circumstance produces a larger decline in mental health and well-being than being involuntarily out of work for six months or more. It is the worst thing that can happen, he says, equivalent to the death of a spouse, and "a kind of bereavement" in its own right. Only a small fraction of the decline can be tied directly to losing a paycheck, Oswald notes; most of it appears to be the result of a tarnished identity and a loss of self-worth. Unemployment leaves psychological scars that remain even after work is found again. And because the happiness of family members is usually closely related, the misery spreads throughout the home.[2]

The social costs of joblessness are difficult to calculate but no less real than those imposed on the personal or individual level. Think about it for a moment: Jobless persons, by definition, are not employed, and therefore we—society at large—lose out on the goods and services that they would produce were they gainfully at work. Joblessness, in other words, imposes a social cost in terms of forgone goods and services—goods and services that, were they available, could enrich our standard of living and help meet unfulfilled needs.

Now, add to this the additional tax revenues that governments would receive if jobless individuals were working; the various forms of income assistance that jobless individuals receive because of their joblessness or reduced incomes; the cost of incarcerating those individuals whose joblessness lead them to engage in criminal activity; and the virulently racist groups that economic misery often spawns, and you begin to get an idea of the staggering social costs associated with widespread joblessness and poverty. So, again, joblessness is no joke—for the jobless themselves or

2. Ibid., 19.

for the rest of us. With regard to Darity, he makes it absolutely clear that he's also keenly concerned about the "adverse health outcomes, both mental and physical, associated with exposure to prolonged unemployment."[3]

The human and social carnage left in the wake of joblessness, then, is one of the justifications that Darity offers in support of his specific policy proposal for wiping out involuntary unemployment and the poverty that often accompanies it. But, as we'll see, the justificatory basis of his response to joblessness goes beyond the notion that we ought to prevent the occurrence of personal and social harm. He also believes that the existence of involuntary joblessness is prima facie evidence that the right to work at decent wages is being violated. And about this, he says, something must be done immediately.

Darity's Proposal for a National Investment Employment Corps

In his 2011 testimony before the Congressional Black Caucus Deficit Commission, Darity began by drawing attention to our current employment crisis:

> The Bureau of Labor Statistics reports that 14.5 million Americans remained in the ranks of the unemployed in December 2010. December's unemployment rate of 9.4 percent represented the twentieth consecutive month where the jobless rate exceeded 9 percent, the longest span with rates that high since the Great Depression. While the December estimate represented a decline in the unemployment rate, it was in part attributable to a decline in the labor force participation rate associated with discouragement effects and the employment-population ratio remained unchanged at 58.3 percent. The nation faces an ongoing and sustained employment crisis.[4]

3. Darity, "Direct Route to Full Employment," 181.
4. Darity, "Insuring Permanent Full Employment," par. 1.

This "ongoing and sustained employment crisis" was not only undermining people's livelihoods and well-being; it was also contributing to the financial fragility of government, making it that much more difficult to find our way out of the economic doldrums: "Having Americans out of work does immense damage to the human spirit, imposes extensive costs to the individual and society as a whole, and creates and perpetuates deficit finance crises at all levels of government—federal, state, and local."[5]

Crushed spirits, personal and social costs, and economic doldrums are serious problems—so serious that Darity is convinced that we ought to—and can—do something about it; we ought to (and can) protect ourselves against the ravages of involuntary joblessness and the socioeconomic misery that accompanies it. And one of the ways in which we can do so is through the creation of what he calls a National Investment Employment Corps (NIEC).

The NIEC, among other things, would put an end to involuntary joblessness by securing full employment and realizing the right to work. More specifically, Darity's proposed NIEC addresses the crisis of joblessness by mandating that the federal government implement a job guarantee program, with the underlying principle being that "the opportunity to work for decent pay is a citizenship right for all Americans."[6] Before further discussing the details and costs of his proposal, it's important to note where the inspiration for that proposal comes from.

The Source of Darity's Vision

His vision here is inspired by at least three significant developments: the New Deal–era's jobs programs, a 1972 study by African-American economists called "An Economic Bill of Rights," and the Full Employment and Balanced Growth Act of 1978, more widely known as the Humphrey-Hawkins Act.

5. Ibid., par. 2.
6. Ibid.

With regard to the New Deal, Darity specifically singles out its Civilian Conservation Corps (CCC). Unlike the CCC, however, the job guarantee that resides at the heart of his NEIC would be permanent; it would be there in both good and bad economic times. This permanency appears to reflect Darity's conviction that the American economy is typically characterized by a shortage of jobs—worse at some times than at others, but always an issue. Here's how he puts it:

> The national government should establish the equivalent of a Civilian Conservation Corps (CCC) similar to the type that employed 3.5 million citizens in 1936, one of the worst years of the Great Depression, But, unlike the CCC, the new public employment service (it could be named the National Investment Employment Corps) would assure every American seeking work that a job is available in either good or bad times. . . . Under a federal job guarantee, the national government would function as an employer of last resort, providing basic job security for all Americans.[7]

And, as I've alluded to above, Darity pays homage to the earlier efforts of a group of African-American scholars who likewise sought to champion and popularize the notion that genuine full employment is achievable by means of insuring the right to work. The work of this group yielded a 1972 report titled "An Economic Bill of Rights."[8] A centerpiece of this bill is the notion that persons have a right to work and that, by maintaining conditions of full employment, the government has the duty to ensure that persons can enjoy or access this right to work.

As for what became known as the Humphrey-Hawkins bill, its original version—the one proposed by Augustus Hawkins (D-CA)—would have guaranteed jobs for all who wanted work. In

7. Darity, "Direct Route to Full Employment," 179.

8. Marcus et al., "Economic Bill of Rights." Darity writes, "On pages 6–13 of the 'Economic Bill of Rights' . . . maintenance of conditions of full employment is advanced as a fundamental right." Darity, "From Here to Full Employment," 3.

fact, if national policies failed to generate full employment, then it fell to the federal government to finance the creation of jobs to take up the slack, with those employed in the federally financed jobs being paid the prevailing wage rate. The federal government, in other words, would serve as the employer of last resort. There was a legal component as well: "[T]he bill made the right to employment legally enforceable, allowing individuals to sue if they were denied a job."[9] While what was ultimately passed is pretty far from what Hawkins initially had in mind, the Humphrey-Hawkins Act of 1976 did mandate the achievement of full employment as one of the guiding goals of national economic policy. Darity's mentioning of the Humphrey-Hawkins Act, then, is best seen as a challenge to policymakers—and indeed an inspiration to all of us—to make the securing of full employment a guiding principle of economic policy.

Having briefly discussed the sources or events that inspire Darity's vision, we can now return to a further explication of the details of his proposed National Investment Employment Corps, as well as the estimated costs that would be associated with the implementation of the NIEC.

A Return to the Specifics

By now it is clear, I hope, that Darity's conception of full employment is inextricably linked with the right to work; to achieve genuine full employment, a situation wherein all who want to work can work, we need to arrange our socioeconomic policies such that there is a guarantee of a decent-paying job for every jobless person who genuinely seeks paid employment. Here are the specifics of Darity's proposal:

- The National Investment Employment Corps would offer a guaranteed job to all jobless citizens who have reached the minimum age of eighteen. The jobs would pay a minimum salary of $20,000, with an additional $10,000 in benefits.

9. Weir, *Politics and Jobs*, 135.

Taking salary and benefits into account, the minimum total compensation per job would be $30,000.

- The jobs must have a useful social function and meet some unmet social needs. States and municipalities would be responsible for assessing their physical and human infrastructure needs. Priority would be given to the "repair, maintenance, and construction of the nation's deteriorating infrastructure."[10] Other potential projects would include training personnel to provide high-quality child care, improving parks and recreation areas, and rejuvenating the nation's struggling postal service. States and municipalities would develop a job bank detailing the most pressing physical and social needs that might be met by the National Investment Employment Corps.

- The program would cost no more than $750 billion. In January 2011, approximately fifteen million persons were officially classified as unemployed. To arrive at a ballpark figure of the cost, Darity assumes that the mean or average expense per worker would be $50,000—a figure that includes salaries, benefits, and materials and equipment. To put all fifteen million unemployed persons to work, then, would cost $750 billion—a figure that, as Darity points out, is lower than the first stimulus package enacted by Congress in an effort to jumpstart the economy.

- A job guarantee program would make it possible to reduce or eliminate our current expenditures on such programs as unemployment insurance and food stamps. With the National Investment Employment Corps, jobs with decent pay would be provided to all of the unemployed. As a consequence, we would, says Darity, be able to substantially reduce, if not completely eliminate, our expenditures on these and similar programs that provide assistance to the jobless poor. The reduction or elimination of these types of programs would represent a savings, and thus the actual cost of the National

10. Darity, "Direct Route to Full Employment," 180.

Investment Employment Corps would be lower—well under the $750 billion figure.

A Recapitulation of the Benefits of a National Investment Employment Corps

I've already mentioned some of the benefits that Darity claims would flow from his National Investment Employment Corps. In addition to those already mentioned above, Darity also notes the following:

- The National Investment Employment Corps would be countercyclical and thereby militate against severe economic slumps. An economic crash or slump always results in increased levels of joblessness and poverty. This, in turn, results in decreased spending on the part of the jobless. Since my spending is your income, if as a result of being jobless I reduce my spending, then your income will be decreased. In the face of your decreased income, you may reduce your spending. But when you do that, someone else's income gets reduced and they reduce their spending. What we end up with, then, is a downward spiral that just gets worse, creating an ever-growing economic hole that we have to dig ourselves out of. By immediately expanding during an economic crisis and thereby putting to work those left jobless as a result of economic recession, a National Investment Employment Corps would short-circuit this process and thereby militate against a cumulative process whereby we sink deeper and deeper into an economic pit.

- The National Investment Employment Corps would shore up the government's fragile tax base. During economic downturns, all levels of government experience a shortage of tax revenues. What makes this particularly nasty is that the tax base dwindles at the very time that increased joblessness results in increased needs. Darity notes that, by guaranteeing work to all those who find themselves jobless, the National

Investment Employment Corps would help restore govern-
mental tax bases that are eroding as a result of economic
slumps.

• The National Investment Employment Corps would provide the assurance of quality jobs for "acutely stigmatized
populations."[11] Perhaps no group is more "stigmatized" than
those who have been incarcerated. Not surprisingly, ex-cons
face tremendous odds when trying to secure employment after their release. This is particularly true for African-Americans with criminal records. It's hard enough trying to land a
job, especially a decent one, when you have a criminal record,
and it's doubly hard if you're black with a criminal record.[12]
Such a failure to secure employment can easily cause many to
return to their former activities and thereby lead to re-incar-
ceration. A job guarantee program, Darity points out, "would
provide employment for all—black or white, male or female,
with a criminal record or without."[13]

• The National Investment Employment Corps would allow the
securing of both full employment and price stability. One of
the most common objections lodged against a policy regime
of guaranteed jobs is that it will result in an upward and perhaps uncontrollable spiral in the general price level. In other
words, the price of the ticket—inflation—makes it too costly
to "purchase" full employment. Darity, however, suggests that
this need not be the case—that we can have both genuine full
employment and price stability: "The Humphrey-Hawkins
Act mandates both full employment and price stability, often
objectives seen as incompatible. But with the government as
the direct employer of the jobless . . . the full employment goal
creates far less inflationary pressure than stimulus packages

11. Darity, "Direct Route to Full Employment," 181.

12. Pager, Marked, esp. 45–60.

13. Darity, "Insuring Permanent Full Employment," par. 8.

and bank bailouts. With the federal job guarantee both demands of the law could be met simultaneously."[14]

So, Darity is one economist who is convinced that we can do better than we're doing now. He believes, as we've just seen, that a program similar to King's own economic bill of rights is just what's needed for our current economic ills. Sure, he calls his proposal a National Investment Employment Corps, but it is, as should be apparent from the previous chapters, a kissing cousin of King's economic bill of rights. But what's really intriguing here is his suggestion that securing genuine full employment and the right to work is not beyond our economic resources. His rough estimate of $750 billion does not capture the increased savings and additional revenues that would be associated with a serious and successful effort to secure the full-employment/right-to-work agenda. Abolish joblessness and you'll get, among other things, stronger families, more resilient communities, more taxpayers, and decreased expenditures on some transfer payments. Whether you call it a National Investment Employment Corps or an economic bill of rights, the possibilities seem promising. And just imagine how promising it would be if we could implement a jobs program of this type without appreciably increasing the deficit—without, that is, going into debt to secure King's dream of full employment and the right to work.

Well, in the next chapter, you'll meet another economist who believes that we can do exactly that.

14. Darity, "From Here to Full Employment," 5.

5

The Contribution of Philip Harvey

An Economic Ethic of Employment Assurance

Over the past two decades, Philip Harvey has emerged as one of the most forceful advocates of the full-employment/right-to-work agenda. Holding a JD from Yale Law School and PhD in economics from the New School for Social Research, Harvey is currently a professor of law and economics at the Rutgers School of Law. And since the publication, in 1989, of his book *Securing the Right to Employment: Social Welfare Policy and the Unemployed in the United States*, he has used his legal and economic skills to refute the claim that securing the right to work and genuine full employment can't be done without unleashing inflationary forces. Harvey argues that we can use a strategy of direct job creation to stamp out the scourge of joblessness and that doing so will not cost nearly as much as is commonly assumed. In fact, it's his contention that, by using a strategy of direct job creation, we can secure full employment and the right to work without appreciably adding to the nation's deficit and debt load.

What Harvey proposes is variously described by the terms "employment assurance program," "direct job creation," "employer of last resort," and "job guarantee." Grounded in the human rights language of the New Deal, as well as in international proclamations of the right to work, Harvey's proposal is a strategy of direct job creation wherein the federal government has the moral obligation of ensuring that all have access to living wage jobs that enable persons to live dignified lives. And, as I've indicated above, he demonstrates that the "price of the ticket" is not nearly as high as is commonly assumed.

To unpack the logic of his argument, I begin by discussing what he considers to be the primary personal and social costs associated with joblessness and its attendant ills. Like King and Darity, Harvey underscores the fact that joblessness is not free, that in fact we pay—both individually and collectively—a considerable sum when we allow millions to languish in poverty. I follow this discussion by highlighting the fundamental sources underlying Harvey's vision, with an emphasis on how his own vision is shaped by the New Deal's vision of human rights and by international proclamations of the right to work. The domestic and international proclamation of the right to work, as we'll see, leads Harvey to incorporate a robust conception of full employment in his strategy of direct job creation—a conception of full employment that entails a quantitative, qualitative, and distributive dimension. Next, I'll turn to what he considers to be the distinct advantages associated with an employment assurance or direct job creation program. And, finally, I'll turn to his estimate of the cost of such a program. It's here that we'll encounter his argument that, yes, it's possible to instantiate the full-employment/right-to-work agenda without appreciably contributing to the nation's deficit and without unleashing unmanageable inflationary forces. The upshot here, of course, is that there are no grounds for presuming that we must sacrifice millions at the altar of joblessness in order to "enjoy" the "gift" of price stability.

The Personal and Social Costs
of Involuntary Joblessness and Poverty

Woven throughout Harvey's work is the theme that joblessness slams its victims with enormous material, physical, and psychological costs. If you're jobless, particularly for a prolonged period, your exposure to poverty is heightened. And, furthermore, poverty's material deprivation is even more intense when it occurs, as Harvey writes, "in the midst of plenty." It's not surprising, then, that joblessness has a way of eroding self-esteem:

> First, unemployment is the primary cause of both absolute and relative poverty. This poverty is harmful because it involves real material deprivation, but it may hurt even more when it's experienced in the midst of plenty. For this reason, poverty caused by jobless-ness during periods of general economic prosperity may be especially damaging to persons who suffer it. This effect is likely to be even more pronounced in a society like the United States where both social status and self-esteem depend heavily on the kind of work one does and how it is rewarded. In fact, being invol-untarily unemployed is a deeply corrosive experience, even when it is not associated with significant material deprivation.[1]

As if that's not bad enough, Harvey reminds us that there is an abundance of evidence indicating that the stress that comes along with joblessness can either cause or exacerbate a host of psy-chological and physical ills:

> In addition to its role in causing poverty, unemploy-ment is associated with a wide range of adverse psy-chological and physical health effects ranging from a loss of self-esteem to increased mortality from a sur-prisingly wide variety of illnesses. The stress associated with being unemployed seems literally to attack our bodies as well as our psyches. Stress is also associated with increased rates of suicide and attempted suicide.[2]

Nor should we forget that joblessness often takes a toll on our most cherished relationships, constantly threatening to undermine our families as well as our emotional connection with our spouses, children, and friends. On this point, Harvey writes the following:

1. Harvey, "Human Rights and Economic Policy Discourse," 398–99.
2. Ibid., 399.

Unemployment causes enormous social harm. It is disruptive of a wide range of relationships—including with spouses, children, and close friends, in addition to more casual acquaintances. As such, unemployment is an enemy of stable family formation and a destroyer of existing families. Not surprisingly, it also causes increased criminal activity and other anti-social behavior.[3]

But if you're employed—and the vast majority of us are, even in economic downturns—you might think that joblessness doesn't really affect you and others like you; you might think, in other words, that you're not paying a cost. Well, Harvey would say you need to think again. Or, more pointedly, Harvey says that all of us—including those who have jobs—pay a cost when our fellow citizens find themselves involuntarily unemployed. For starters, as a society we lose out on the goods and services that the jobless would produce were they employed. We also incur a cost in the form of income assistance to the jobless, which helps them cope with the material deprivation associated with joblessness and the poverty that it often produces or exacerbates. There *is* a social cost or price to pay as a result of joblessness. So, if you think the cost of poverty is strictly confined to the individual level, here's what Harvey has to say to you:

> The portion of the population that does not suffer un-
> employment directly—and even in the deepest reces-
> sion they comprise the vast majority of workers at any
> moment in time—also suffers negative utilities due to
> the unemployment of others. The economic costs that
> society bears as a result of the problem include the fore-
> gone goods and services that jobless individuals would
> have produced if they had been employed (including
> the forgone taxes they would have paid), the cost of
> charitable gifts and transfer payments made to jobless
> individuals as a result of their joblessness by both in-
> dividuals and governments, and a plethora of indirect

3. Ibid., 400.

costs borne by society as result of the health and social problems caused or aggravated by the problem.[4]

At first glance, it might seem that Harvey's argument is essentially a straightforward appeal to self-interest—an argument that based on the costs and benefits, an eradication of involuntary joblessness would increase society's aggregate utility. And while he does acknowledge that it is possible to launch a utilitarian-based argument in favor of eradicating involuntary joblessness, he is also quick to point out that we need not—and should not—limit arguments in favor of genuine full employment to utilitarian bases. As he sees it, the ultimate issue is one of human rights and not simply one of discretionary public policy. He accepts and defends the idea that humans qua humans have a right to jobs at decent pay. Thus, he views the government's failure to pursue the full-employment/right-to-work agenda as a human rights violation. Indeed, and as I'll demonstrate below, his vision of the good society is one that actively seeks to support and secure what he considers to be the right of all persons to jobs at decent pay. Prior to outlining Harvey's vision, however, let me quote a passage from his *Securing the Right to Employment*, one that provides an entreé into comprehending the central argument that runs throughout his work:

> I argue that self-interest alone should direct the nation to adopt measures securing the right to employment, and my study may therefore be regarded as an effort to address the concerns of conventional policy analysis. At the same time, however, it is also possible to view my study as an effort to advance a human rights claim that effective governmental action to secure the right to employment is morally and possibly even legally obligatory in the United States.[5]

He continues:

---

4. Ibid., 400–401.
5. Harvey, *Securing the Right to Employment*, 9–10.

In other words, the case for recognizing the right to employment can be made strictly on utilitarian grounds, but it need not be limited to such arguments alone. Moreover, if a legitimate human rights claim can be made, then both political and moral considerations argue for making that claim as forcefully as possible. Consider, for example, the history of the civil rights movement in the United States. It would certainly have been possible to argue for an end to racial discrimination strictly on utilitarian grounds. Neoclassical economic theory suggests that such discrimination is economically irrational. Does anyone believe, though, that it would have been politically wise for the civil rights movement to have limited itself to such arguments? More pointedly, does anyone believe that it would have been morally acceptable for the country to tolerate slavery, or school segregation, or employment discrimination, if such practices could in fact have been shown to be more "efficient" than nondiscriminatory ones?[6]

Basic Sources of Harvey's Vision

The New Deal as a Source of Harvey's Vision of the Good Society

Harvey's vision of the good society is inspired and shaped by the domestic and international human rights movement, with a particular emphasis on the way that that movement eventually found expression in the New Deal's strategy to stamp out involuntary joblessness and to secure full employment via the strategy of direct job creation. More directly, the social welfare strategy proposed by the New Deal's Committee on Economic Security (CES) and the National Resources Planning Board (NRPB), as well as the Universal Declaration of Human Rights, provides the moral principles

6. Ibid., 10.

that guide Harvey's own proposal for eradicating the twin problems of joblessness and poverty.[7]

As a presidential task force chaired by Secretary of Labor Francis Perkins, the CES was given the responsibility of developing legislative proposals "to promote greater economic security" for the American people. In its January 1935 report to the president, the CES described its goals thus:

> The one almost all-embracing measure of security is an assured income. A program of economic security, as we envision it, must have as its primary aim the assurance of an adequate income to each human being in childhood, youth, middle age, or old age—in sickness or in health. It must provide safeguards against all of the hazards leading to destitution and dependency.[8]

To accomplish this goal, the committee proposed what Harvey calls a "two-legged social welfare strategy": One leg deals with the income needs of the jobless by way of the assurance of employment, while the other leg would provide income to those who, whether temporarily or permanently, could not or were not expected to support themselves through paid work in the regular labor market.[9] And that first leg, the one of employment assurance, was envisioned as a permanent feature of the social welfare landscape. It would be there in good as well as dire economic times. As the CES put it,

> Since most people live by work, the first objective in a program of economic security must be maximum employment. As the major contribution of the Federal Government in providing a safeguard against unemployment we suggest employment assurance—the stimulation of private employment and the provision

7. Harvey, "Human Rights and Economic Policy Discourse," esp. 371–87.

8. U.S. Congress, *Economic Security*, 23–24.

9. As part of the second leg, the CES proposed, among other things, the nation's present Social Security system, as well as Old Age Assistance, Unemployment Insurance, and AID for Dependent Children (later renamed Aid for Families with Dependent Children).

of public employment for those able-bodied workers whom industry cannot employ at a given time. Public work programs are most necessary in periods of severe depression, but may be needed in normal times, as well, to help meet the problems of stranded communities or declining industries.[10]

You'll notice that, among other things, the CES report does not invoke the language of human rights. Yet, the 1942 report produced by the NRPB picks up on the theme of economic security raised by the CES and translates it into the language of human rights. Headed by Frederic Delano, President Roosevelt's uncle, the NRPB "was charged with developing new ideas and experiments, with the goal of promoting employment and economic security."[11] With the winding down of World War II, the NRPB was also involved in "post-defense planning," with an eye toward taking steps to ensure that the postwar period would not be characterized by the return of the levels of joblessness and economic misery that characterized the Great Depression.

In any case, what really grabs Harvey's attention and shapes his proposed strategy for a definitive end to joblessness is the way in which the NRPB's 1942 report links the struggle against joblessness with the realization of human rights. Of particular interest to Harvey, of course, is the connection that the report makes between the abolition of joblessness, full employment, and the right to work. As far as the NRPB is concerned, the securing of full employment is so vital—so critical to peace, justice, and democracy—that it should be the declared policy of the federal government to "insure jobs at decent pay to all those able to work."[12] And, as I've already mentioned, the report ties the achievability of full employment to the securing of the right to work at decent pay. Thus, in the list of the proposed rights contained in the report, the first three read as follows:

10. U.S. Congress, *Economic Security*, 23–24.
11. Sunstein, *Second Bill of Rights*, 85.
12. Cited in Quigly, *Ending Poverty*, 107.

1. The right to work, usefully and creatively through the productive years;

2. The right to fair pay, adequate to command the necessities
   and amenities of life in exchange for work, ideas, thrift, and
   other socially valuable service;

3. The right to adequate food, clothing, shelter, and medical
   care.

To secure these rights, the NRPB not only proposes such things as
a strengthened social security system and a national health care
plan, but, of equal importance, it calls for the establishment of a
permanent policy of direct job creation for all those unable to find
employment in the regular job market. In its report, it is the federal
government that has the ultimate "responsibility for insuring jobs
at decent pay to all those able to work regardless of whether they
can pass a means test." But, expressing a principle that also figures
prominently in Harvey's work, the NRPB makes it abundantly
clear that any publicly provided work must meet some pressing
social need. In other words, the jobs must be "socially useful" and
"arranged according to the variety of abilities and locations of persons seeking work."[13]

Roosevelt's Call for a Second Bill of Rights

Perhaps there is no more poignant expression of the New Deal's
vision of human rights than that found in President Roosevelt's
January 1944 State of the Union address. As previously mentioned, Cass Sunstein dubs it "the greatest speech of the twentieth
century."[14] What makes it so outstanding, according to Sunstein, is
not its elegance—the speech itself, he says, was "messy, sprawling,
unruly, a bit of a pastiche, and not at all literary"; in his judgment, it
was "the opposite of Lincoln's tight, poetic Gettysburg Address."[15]
So what, then, is its claim to "greatness"? To this question, Sun-

13. Ibid.
14. Sunstein, *Second Bill of Rights*, 10.
15. Ibid.

stein's answer is simple and direct: "But because of what it said, it has a strong claim to being the greatest speech of the twentieth century."[16]

Harvey would undoubtedly find little to quibble with here. While he does not claim, as does Sunstein, that Roosevelt's 1944 speech can legitimately be called "the greatest speech of the twentieth century," he clearly considers it to be of supreme importance. In Harvey's eyes, the speech—as I've indicated above—is a sort of capstone statement of the New Deal's vision of the centrality of full employment and human rights to the realization of a fair, peaceful, and democratic community:

> In 1944, with the end of war in sight, Roosevelt chose to use his State of the Union Message to summarize his argument that the employment and social welfare entitlements his administration had sought to secure were in fact human rights that the federal government had a duty to secure.[17]

More pointedly, Roosevelt glances back at the nation's original Bill of Rights and finds that the rights it enshrined, though of critical importance, are "inadequate"—they do not assure economic security for individuals. Because of his conviction that "true individual freedom cannot exist without economic security and independence," Roosevelt calls for a "second Bill of Rights under which a new basis of security and prosperity can be established for all—regardless of station, race, or creed."[18] In a refinement of the earlier list submitted by the NRPB, Roosevelt ticks off eight rights, including the following three rights:

- The right to a useful and remunerative job in the industries or shops or farms or mines of the Nation;

- The right to earn enough to provide adequate food and clothing and recreation;

16. Ibid.
17. Harvey, "Why Is the Right to Work So Hard to Secure?," 151.
18. Cited in Sunstein, *Second Bill of Rights*, 242–43.

- The right to adequate protection from the economic fears of old age, sickness, accident, and unemployment.

And, as Harvey correctly observes, this vision of human rights—including the right to a job at decent pay—had a profound influence on the international level.[19] Harvey cites the United Nations Charter, the Universal Declaration of Human Rights, and the International Covenant on Economic, Social, and Cultural Rights as the primary international sources of his vision of the good society.[20]

The United Nations Charter

Drafted in 1945, the United Nations Charter is an international treaty that imposes binding obligations on member states under international law. Harvey begins his analysis by focusing on Articles 55 and 56 of the Charter:

Article 55

With a view to the creation of conditions of stability and well-being which are necessary for peaceful and friendly relations among the nations based in respect for the principle of equal rights and self-determination of peoples, the United Nations shall promote:

a. higher standards of living, full employment and conditions of economic and social progress and development;

b. solutions of international economic, social, health, and related problems, and international cultural and educational co-operation; and,

19. Harvey, "Why Is the Right to Work So Hard to Secure?," 156.

20. Harvey, "Human Rights and Economic Policy Disclosure," esp. 371–80.

c. universal respect for, and observance of, human rights and fundamental freedoms for all without distinction as to race, sex, language, or religion.

Article 56

All members pledge themselves to take joint and separate action in co-operation with the Organization for the achievement of the purposes set forth in Article 55.[21]

As Harvey notes, the United States—as a member state—is under obligation to promote both full employment and human rights. And while the Charter itself does not define the substance or concept of human rights, Harvey notes that "the nature of the 'full employment' goal that is the subject of this obligation is fairly clear."[22] In particular, he posits that "the nature of the full employment goal" is grounded in an understanding that predominated in the 1940s: "[Full employment] describes a state of affairs in which adequately paid work is available to all job seekers."[23] This understanding of full employment is aptly defined by William Beveridge, widely considered the father of the British welfare state. Of full employment, Beveridge writes,

> It means having always more vacant jobs than unemployed men, not slightly fewer jobs. It means that the jobs are at fair wages, of such a kind, and so located that the unemployed men can reasonably be expected to take them; means, by consequence, that the normal lag between losing one job and finding another will be very short.[24]

Likewise, a 1949 United Nations task force, led by the American economist John Maurice Clark, endorsed a similar

21. Cited in ibid., 372–73.
22. Ibid., 373.
23. Ibid.
24. Beveridge, *Full Employment*, 18.

understanding of the "nature of full employment," defining it as "a situation in which unemployment does not exceed the minimum allowances that must be made for the effects of frictional and seasonal factors."[25] In practical terms, Clark and his fellow researchers thought that full employment translated into an aggregate unemployment rate of 2 percent.

The Universal Declaration of Human Rights

As is well known, the commission that drafted the Universal Declaration of Human Rights was chaired by none other than Eleanor Roosevelt, an official U.S. delegate to the United Nations from 1946 to 1952 and the first elected chair of the United Nations Human Rights Commission. Echoing the New Deal vision of human rights, Article 23 of the Universal Declaration of Human Rights reads as follows:

(1) Everyone has the right to work, to free choice of employment, to just and favorable conditions of work and to protection against unemployment.

(2) Everyone, without any discrimination, has the right to equal pay for equal work.

(3) Everyone who works has the right to just and favorable remuneration insuring for himself and his family an existence worthy of human dignity, and supplemented, if necessary, by other means of social protection.

(4) Everyone has the right to form and to join trade unions for the protection of his interest.[26]

Harvey maintains that, although not a "legally binding agreement under international law," the Universal Declaration "articulates the common understanding of the peoples of the world concerning the substantive content of the human rights that

25. Clark et al., *National and International Measures*, 13.
26. Cited in Sunstein, *Second Bill of Rights*, 245.

members of the United Nations have a legally binding obligation to promote under Articles 55 and 56 of the organization's Charter."[27] From Harvey's perspective, at least one additional comment on the significance of Article 23 is warranted. Consider the phrase "protection against unemployment." To "protect" against unemployment, says Harvey, does not mean to provide "social welfare" so that the victims of joblessness can survive its consequences. It does not mean the cobbling together and provision of funds to persons *after* they have been hit by joblessness. It means, according to Harvey, taking active measures to prevent the occurrence of involuntary joblessness; it means making concerted efforts to bring to fruition full employment and the principle of the right to work. "It should be understood," Harvey writes, "that the drafters of the document clearly understood 'protection against unemployment' to mean protection against the occurrence of involuntary unemployment, and not just the provision of social welfare benefits to protect the victims of unemployment from its harmful consequences." He then goes on to say that the document's drafters "also clearly understood that the obligation to strive to achieve the right to work encompassed the obligation to achieve full employment recognized in Articles 55 and 56 of the United Nations Charter."[28] For Harvey, then, part of the significance here is that a link is made between the securing of full employment and the struggle to promote and protect the right to employment.

The International Covenant on Economic, Social, and Cultural Rights

Because the Universal Declaration of Human Rights was not "originally perceived as imposing binding obligations on governments,"[29] two international treaties, the International Covenant on Civil and Political Rights (ICCPR) and the International

---

27. Harvey, "Securing the Right to Work," 5.
28. Harvey, "Human Rights and Economic Policy Discourse," 376–77.
29. Ibid., 377.

Covenant on Economic, Social, and Cultural Rights (ICESCR), were subsequently drafted to rectify this situation.[30] Articles 6 and 7 of the ICESCR figure prominently in Harvey's own thinking about full employment, the right to work, and the struggle against joblessness. The Articles read as follows:

Article 6

1. The States Parties to the present Covenant recognize the right to work, which includes the right of everyone to the opportunity to gain his living by work which he freely chooses or accepts, and will take appropriate steps to safeguard this right.

2. The steps to be taken by a State Party to the present Covenant to achieve the full realization of this right shall include technical and vocational guidance and training programs, policies and techniques to achieve steady economic, social and cultural development and full and productive employment under conditions safeguarding fundamental political and economic freedoms to the individual.

Article 7

The States Parties to the present Covenant recognize the right of everyone to the enjoyment of just and favorable conditions of work which ensure, in particular:

(a) Remuneration which provides all workers, as a minimum, with:

(i) Fair wages and equal remuneration for work of equal value without distinction of any kind,

---

30. Siegel, *Employment and Human Rights*, esp. 52–71. Both Covenants were signed by President Carter in 1977 and then forwarded to the Senate for ratification. While the Senate ratified the ICCPR in 1992, it has yet to ratify the ICESCR. As a result, the United States remains exempt from the monitoring and enforcement standards established under the ICESCR.

in particular women being guaranteed conditions of work not inferior to those enjoyed by
men, with equal pay for equal work;

(ii) A decent living for themselves and their families in accordance with the provisions of the
present Covenant;

(b) Safe and healthy working conditions;

(c) Equal opportunity for everyone to be promoted
in his employment to an appropriate higher level,
subject to no considerations other than those of
seniority and competence;

(d) Rest, leisure and reasonable limitation of working
hours and periodic holidays with pay, as well as
remuneration for public holidays.[31]

Although the United States Senate has never ratified the
ICESCR, Harvey reminds us that the rights proclaimed in the
covenant are essentially identical with the proclamation contained
in the Universal Declaration, which leads him to conclude that
"to the extent that the United Nations Charter and the Universal
Declaration already bind the United States, our failure to ratify the
ICESCR does not diminish our government's obligation to strive
to achieve full employment and to provide protection for the right
to work."[32]

Implications for the Definitions of Full Employment and the Right to Work

The New Deal's vision of human rights, the United Nations Charter, the United Nations Declaration of Human Rights, and the
International Covenant on Economic, Social, and Cultural Rights
all come together to form a specific conception or definition of

31. Cited in ibid., 242–43.
32. Harvey, "Human Rights and Economic Policy Discourse," 378.

full employment and the right to work. According to Harvey, these sources reveal that the full-employment/right-to-work agenda is multidimensional,[33] by which he means that the full-employment/right-to-work agenda is quantitative, qualitative, and distributive in nature. Quantitatively, the securing of the full-employment/right-to-work agenda requires that the number of jobs available be ample enough to provide employment opportunities for all job seekers. This is important, first of all, because the sources underlying Harvey's vision describe full employment as that situation wherein jobs are available for all job seekers. For obvious reasons, a shortage of jobs undermines efforts to secure full employment, and it also undercuts any genuine effort to promote and protect the right to work. More formally, it boils down to this: in order to realize the full-employment/right-to-work agenda, the number of job vacancies must be at least as great as the number of persons seeking jobs. On this point, Harvey makes the following observation:

> The quantitative aspect is . . . intended to protect the right of job seekers actually to be employed in freely chosen jobs, not simply to compete on terms of equality for scarce employment opportunities. Securing the right accordingly requires that the number of jobs available to persons in an economy exceed the number of persons wanting paid employment, that those jobs be of a type suited to the skills of the labor force, and that no barriers exist which would prevent job seekers from filling those jobs. This condition is what the term full employment was understood to mean when it first gained popular currency in the 1940s.[34]

But there's more to it than this. Let's suppose, for instance, that there is an explosion in the absolute number of jobs and that, as a result, the number of job vacancies far exceeds the number of job seekers. If, however, that explosion leads to an avalanche of low-quality jobs, then the standards of the full-employment/

33. Harvey, "Benchmarking the Right to Work," 123.
34. Ibid.

right-to-work agenda would remain unmet. Even a cursory review of the aforementioned sources reveals references to such "quality" issues as decent pay, safe working conditions, and the right to unionize. To reiterate, the achievability of the full-employment/right-to-work agenda requires a qualitative as well as a quantitative dimension.

> The qualitative aspect of the right to work includes those factors which determine whether a particular job qualifies as "decent work" . . . These factors define the terms and conditions of a particular job—including such things as pay, fringe benefits, hours of work, working conditions, workplace governance, employment security, and so forth. For the right to work to be secured, it is not enough that the number of jobs available in an economy exceed the number of job seekers. Those jobs must provide "decent work." This means that a particular job must satisfy certain minimum standards to be counted as securing a particular individual's right to work.[35]

For Harvey, then, the full-employment/right-to-work agenda strives to achieve both a *right to work*—the quantitative dimension—and *rights at work*—the qualitative dimension. Anything less than that does not secure full employment and the right to work, at least not as it is envisioned in the sources that support Harvey's vision of the good society.

But what about the distributive dimension of the full-employment/right-to-work agenda? This dimension underscores the importance of the principles of equal employment opportunity and nondiscrimination. As conceived by Harvey, any barrier that prevents certain demographic groups from accessing employment opportunities and that fosters unequal treatment on the job constitutes a moral transgression against the fundamental standards of the full-employment/right-to-work agenda, especially the norms

35. Ibid.

of equal treatment and equal employment opportunity. On this point, he writes:

> Just as the operational content of the right to work reflects the Universal Declaration's overarching commitment to the free development of the human personality, so too does it reflect the Declaration's equally strong commitment to the equal worth and equal rights of all persons. This means that the achievement of equal employment opportunity and equal conditions of employment for all persons—regardless of such differentiating characteristics as their race, gender, religion, national origin, political opinion, social class, or other analogous status—is also essential to secure the right to work.[36]

A Strategy of Direct Jobs Creation: Structure, Cost, and Advantage

As a response to the problem of joblessness and the ills that often accompany it, Harvey proposes a strategy of direct job creation that is guided by the various proclamations upholding the right to work and that incorporates the quantitative, qualitative, and distributive dimensions of the full-employment/right-to-work agenda.

Quantitatively, Harvey takes a peek at the historical performance of the U.S. economy and concludes that it is characterized by a perennial jobs gap—a chasm between the number of job vacancies and the number of job seekers. While the size of the gap is larger in bad times than in good times, it is always there, so to speak. So, although the gap increased during the Great Recession—the economic pit that we're currently trying to dig ourselves out of—"the economy had a persistent if much smaller job gap before the recession."[37] To reiterate, Harvey finds that a positive job gap is "an endemic feature of the American labor market—even at

36. Ibid., 124.
37. Harvey, "Securing the Right to Work," 2.

the top of the business cycle."[38] And, what's more, he notes that the burden of the job gap consistently and disproportionately falls on the already weary shoulders of people and communities of color.[39] For Harvey, then, we're sorely in need of a employment assurance program (EAP) that not only closes this gap but is also supportive of racial justice. Drawing on the experience of the New Deal's job creation efforts—and cognizant of the private sector's inability to guarantee genuine full employment—Harvey concludes that an employment assurance program is exactly what we need to close the perennial job gap.

What type of jobs would an EAP provide? For starters, says Harvey, we could begin by putting the jobless to work repairing physical and human infrastructure, as well as identifying and filling the unmet needs of specific communities. Examples include providing high-quality child care and elderly care, rehabbing substandard or abandoned housing, repairing the nation's tattered roads, staffing schools with additional teachers and classroom aides, and so forth. As far as Harvey is concerned, then, there is plenty of work that can be done—work that meets some of our most pressing physical and social needs. He does contend, however, that all job creation efforts must take into account two economic constraints and one political constraint. Economically, the created jobs must take into account the skills of the jobless as well as the needs of various communities, and the jobs must be relatively labor intensive. Politically, efforts must be made to ensure that EAP jobs do not overlap with those that already exist in the public and private sectors:

> The selection of program projects and activities, other than those required for the operation of the program itself, would be subject to two economic constraints and one political constraint. The first economic constraint is that the jobs should be chosen with an eye to the occupational skills and interests of the program's

38. Ibid., 3.

39. Ibid. Here Harvey takes note of the well-known fact that the African-American joblessness rate is typically twice as high as the rate for Whites.

workforce. The second is that the jobs should be relatively labor intensive in order to increase the number of jobs created with the available funding. The political constraint is that the projects and activities selected should avoid conflicts, to the extent reasonably possible, with employers and workers who do similar work in either the regular public or private sectors.[40]

In terms of the qualitative and distributive dimensions, the program participants would receive a wage that is equivalent to what persons with similar skills and qualifications could expect to receive outside of the EAP. For example:

> Unemployed school teachers would receive the same wage that school teachers with similar educational backgrounds, skills and experience receive when they are employed. Unemployed factory workers would receive the same wage that factory workers with similar educational backgrounds, skills and experience receive when they are employed. And high school drop-outs entering the labor market for the first time would receive the same wage that similarly qualified and experienced individuals receive when they are employed.[41]

While this approach upholds the distributive principle of equal pay for equal work, it does not guarantee—as Harvey well knows—that the wages received by EAP participants would enable them to live "dignified lives." Just think about one of the examples offered by Harvey, namely, the high school dropout who is entering the labor market for the first time. Because this person's EAP wage is pegged to what a "similarly qualified" person would earn "outside" of the program, we know that this person's earnings are going to be pretty wretched; no matter how you look at it, high school dropouts simply don't rake in the bucks. On its face, then, Harvey's proposal—at least in some cases—might satisfy a distributive principle while trampling upon some qualitative ones. After

40. Ibid., 21.

41. Harvey, "Back to Work," 15.

all, the sources underlying his vision consistently underscore the importance of living wages—wages that put people on a trajectory to live a life consistent with human dignity. So, how does Harvey deal with this problem?

What he says in response to this problem is this: We have to be willing, if necessary, to supplement the low earnings of some workers with a host of public benefits. More directly, public benefits could and should be used to ensure that all workers receive the functional equivalent of a living wage: "Whether a jobs program that paid market wages could guarantee people what progressives refer to as a 'living wage' depends on the availability of employee benefits and wage supplements for those workers who need them."[42] Some wage supplements that could prove critical to low-wage earners are low- to no-cost child care, the Earned Income Tax Credit (EITC), and housing assistance. To reiterate, Harvey believes that we ought to use public benefits to ensure that the lowest earners are able to enjoy what would, in effect, amount to a living wage.

At this point, you might be asking yourself, how in the world can we possibly afford something like this? Sounds great, but what's the price of the ticket? And if you've been hanging out with certain economists, you might even be thinking that what Harvey's proposing will only end up increasing the nation's deficit and initiating an inflationary spiral. In the very next section, we'll see just how Harvey answers these cost concerns and why he's able to make—and support—the provocative argument that an EAP could very well cost much less than you might think and that a strategy of direct job creation will not set off an unmanageable inflationary spiral.

42. Ibid., 16.

The Price of the Ticket: The Estimated Cost
of a Strategy of Direct Job Creation

Over the past couple of decades or so, Harvey has provided several estimates of what it would cost to implement an employment assurance program—a program by which the feds would assure living wage jobs to all job seekers. This program, by definition, would move the nation toward genuine full employment. Following Harvey's logic, you can also think of it as a strategy for substantially reducing, if not outright eliminating, the job gap that is so characteristic of the U.S. economy.

To appreciate Harvey's estimates, you have to make a distinction between gross and net costs. The gross cost is the price that stares us in the face prior to taking into account any revenue generation and savings that would result from implementing an employment assurance program. The net cost, then, takes into account revenue and savings that would result from implementing the full-employment/right-to-work agenda. In the final analysis, it is the net cost that represents the actual price of the ticket for "purchasing" a policy regime predicated upon full employment and the principle of the right to work.

Harvey begins by noting something that is often overlooked in public discourse concerning the eradication of joblessness and poverty. Harvey frames this as follows:

> Developed market societies provide a range of income transfer benefits to officially unemployed workers, to impoverished individuals who want work whether or not they are counted as unemployed, and to the dependents of both of these groups. For simplicity, I shall refer to all these benefit recipients as the "Unemployed." If a JG [job guarantee] was used to close the economy's job gap, government spending would be reduced for existing transfer benefits to the Unemployed.[43]

43. Harvey, "Funding a Job Guarantee," 121.

So, the first point to note, says Harvey, is that the implementation of an EAP or job guarantee program would bring about an immediate savings in the form of reduced transfer payments to the formerly jobless. What's more, the transformation of transfer benefits into wage payments means that, right off the bat, a significant portion of the EAP wage payments would already be accounted for:

> If those savings totaled "X" billion dollars, the first "X" billion spent on the JG program would already be accounted for. Not only would it not be associated with any change in aggregate demand or deficit spending, it would not be associated with any change in the level of government spending. The only change would be the transformation of transfer benefits into wage payments.[44]

To reiterate, Harvey's argument is that the transformation of transfer benefits into wage payments covers a portion of the cost that would be associated with starting an employment assurance program that would move us toward the goal of full employment and respect for the right to work. But it doesn't end there. When the jobless are transformed into wage earners, they become taxpayers, generating—as do all taxpayers—a stream of revenues:

> Another portion of the budgetary cost of providing a job guarantee would be covered by additional tax receipts attributable to the aforementioned benefits (which generally are not treated as taxable income) into taxable wage income. Program costs covered by this source also would not be associated with any change in aggregate demand or deficit spending, even though it would appear as additional government spending balanced by an equal increase in government revenues.[45]

So, again, here's Harvey's major point: to figure out the "real" or net cost of an employment assurance program, we would have

44. Ibid.
45. Ibid.

to subtract from the budgeted or gross costs the savings in transfer benefits and the additional tax revenues that would result from implementing an EAP.

Harvey follows this procedure to estimate what it would have cost to implement an EAP during the 1977–1986 decade.[46] And what does he find? Over that ten-year period, the budgeted cost would have been approximately $1.2 trillion. That's clearly not chump change. But, significantly, he estimates that during the same period we would have saved about $725 billion in transfer benefit expenditures and generated about $246 billion in income and payroll taxes. In other words, as he points out, "approximately $971 billion or 82 percent of the program's budget cost would have been covered without resort to additional funding sources or deficit spending."[47] So the additional revenues that would have been generated as a result of the unemployed securing jobs and becoming taxpayers, coupled with the savings resulting from the transformation of transfer payments into wages, would have covered the vast majority of the cost of an EAP program.

Furthermore, Harvey reminds us that we need to keep in mind the previously discussed personal and social costs associated with joblessness: higher rates of suicide, the dissolution of families, upticks in homelessness, increases in the number of incarcerated persons, and so forth. To the extent that the eradication of joblessness reduces these costs, we get an additional, although indirect, source of savings. Taking such indirect savings into account further reduces the net cost of an employment assurance program and raises the intriguing possibility that it can be financed without adding to the deficit or initiating an inflationary spiral.

Before concluding this chapter, it would be worthwhile to glance at the results of one of Harvey's more recent efforts to estimate the cost of an employment assurance program that strives to bring about genuine full employment and to promote the right to work at livable wages. You will notice that the figures are different, but that's to be expected. In the first case we looked at the

46. Harvey, *Securing the Right to Employment*, esp. 21–50.
47. Harvey, "Funding a Job Guarantee," 122.

1977–1986 decade; in this case, we will look at 2010, during which we were still trying to dig ourselves out of the Great Recession. Despite these differences, however, the basic conclusion is the same: We can end involuntary joblessness at a very reasonable cost, and we can do so without fueling an inflationary spiral.

A Recent Estimate of the Ticket Price

In a 2011 policy brief, Harvey provided an estimate of what it would have cost, using a strategy of direct job creation, to create one million EAP jobs in 2010. His estimate of the gross cost is $46.4 billion. That gross cost, by the way, includes such "items" as the annual wage bill, the cost of providing federal health benefits to all program participants, and such nonlabor costs as materials and supplies.[48] Yet, according to Harvey, such a response to joblessness would generate additional revenue and savings of $17.8 billion, bringing the net cost of the program down to $28.6 billion. And, Harvey reminds us, don't forget that the net cost does not take into account the types of indirect savings discussed above. Neither does it take into account that when the program participants spend their earnings on goods and services, they actually help spur job creation in the private sector. Indeed, he finds that such spending ends up generating an additional 414,000 jobs outside of the program itself.[49]

Based on his current estimates, he finds that we could almost immediately lower our current unemployment rate to 4.5 percent—the prerecession level—at a net cost of about $235 billion. That represents about 8.2 million additional jobs. And, while that's definitely a nice chunk of change, Harvey offers the following perspective:

> If the Bush-era tax cuts had been allowed to expire at the end of 2010, the federal government would have collected about $295 billion in additional revenue

48. Harvey, "Back to Work," 11.
49. Ibid.

during 2011. This would have been more than enough to cover the cost of the jobs program. Moreover, using the Bush-era tax cut money in this way also would increase employment outside the program by an additional 3.1 million. If those jobs became self-sustaining—as it is reasonable to hope they would—then during 2012, the jobs program would need to provide only 5.1 million jobs to keep the unemployment rate at 4.5 percent. The net cost of providing those jobs would be about $147 billion, while tax collections, if the Bush-era tax cuts had been allowed to expire, would be about $322 billion higher, more than twice as much as would be needed to fund the jobs program that year.[50]

His point? That it lies within our power to launch a massive and direct attack on joblessness and that it need not cost as much as is commonly assumed; in fact, there is reason to believe that it can be funded in such a way that it neither adds to our current deficit nor contributes to an unmanageable inflationary spiral. For Harvey, it's clear that involuntary joblessness is straight-up noxious and that when you have the power to eradicate a "noxious substance," that is what you ought to do. Sure, you can spread it around, distribute it so that it's more evenly shared. But why settle for dilution, Harvey asks, when we can do so much more?

> If given a choice between eliminating an unwanted burden and redistributing its weight so that everyone bears an equal share, who wouldn't choose to eliminate the burden? Diluting a noxious substance may reduce its harmful environmental effects, but not as surely or as well as eliminating it from the environment entirely. Unless good reasons can be cited for not pursuing the goal of full employment, it is an inherently more desirable objective than the equalization of rates of joblessness across population groups.[51]

---

50. Ibid., 12.
51. Harvey, "Combatting Joblessness," 754–55.

With that said, we're now in a position to bring everything together and to draw some conclusions regarding how all of the foregoing might help clarify the economic prerequisites of King's beloved community.

6

The Full-Employment/Right-to-Work Agenda

Lessons Learned

This brief study has reviewed the economic ethic of Dr. Martin Luther King, Jr. and has sought to bring that ethic into contact or conversation with the arguments of two economists who, like King, are convinced that the realization of the full-employment/ right-to-work agenda is the most ethically fitting response to involuntary joblessness and the host of personal and social ills that so often accompany it. I have argued that a particular conception of full employment resides at the heart of the economic prerequisites of King's beloved community, and via reference to the works of economists William Darity and Philip Harvey, I have also sought to provide compelling reasons for believing in the achievability of the full-employment/right-to-work agenda. In the remainder of this chapter, I'll highlight some of the lessons that can be learned from this study, as well as the problems and possibilities that advocates of a Kingian response to joblessness can expect to encounter.

What Lessons Can We Learn?

We can learn several lessons by bringing King's voice into conversation with economists like William Darity and Philip Harvey. For starters: this conversation enables us to flesh out and systematize a conception of full employment that is implicit in and runs throughout King's body of work. Using Harvey's terminology, we would definitely be correct in saying that King's conception of the full-employment/right-to-work agenda is quantitative, qualitative, and distributive in nature. Examine it from whatever angle you will, it's abundantly clear that he understood full employment to mean more than having enough jobs to absorb all job seekers. For King—as for Harvey and Darity—it also means having jobs at livable wages, with safe working conditions and the right of workers to unionize. And, lest we forget about the distributive dimension, it also means working assiduously to dismantle any and all barriers that might impede the access of certain groups and communities to decent employment conditions. Full employment for King, then, means both the right to work and rights at work. It is this conception of full employment—one that goes back at least as far as the New Deal era—that anchors the economic prerequisites of King's beloved community.

Lesson number two is this: the cost of doing nothing is much higher than you might think. Whenever a massive jobs program is proposed, particularly one that is predicated on securing full employment and the right to work, some folks will invariably start hollering about the cost—that is, screaming about how we can't afford it. On the one hand, they're onto something; since few things are free, we may very well have to dig into our collective pockets to make the beloved community's economic prerequisites a reality. In the midst of all the hollering and hand-wringing, however, what is often forgotten is that there is a cost to doing nothing—a cost, in the case of the United States, to allowing millions of our sisters and brothers to remain "members" in the ranks of the unemployed. We pay in terms of broken families, foregone output, shattered relationships, stressful lives, dashed dreams, rising crime rates, and a host of physical and mental ailments. King knew as much, and as we've seen, he never pulled any punches when discussing the personal and social costs of joblessness. Yet, nowhere does he systematically calculate and compare the cost of doing nothing versus the cost of doing something. This should not be surprising; after all, he was a preacher and human rights activist, not an economist. But it is precisely on this point that Darity and Harvey function as an important resource—and corrective—for those who cherish and strive to bring to fruition the economic ideals of King's beloved community. By estimating the savings and additional revenues that would be associated with a jobs guarantee program, Darity and Harvey provide strong reasons for concluding that the cost of doing something about joblessness is substantially less than the cost of maintaining the status quo. More pointedly, their analyses indicate that a strategy of direct job creation—the precise type of policy favored by King—is far from a financial pipe dream; rather, it is fiscally feasible and therefore affordable. Going forward, advocates of King's approach to conquering joblessness would be well served to emphasize the findings of scholars such as Darity and Harvey.

As for the third lesson, it is this: starting from different premises doesn't necessarily mean we can't arrive at the same conclusion. To see what I mean by this, recall and compare the discussions of King's, Darity's, and Harvey's proposals for the eradication of involuntary joblessness. Take, for starters, King's call for an economic bill of rights. For him, as we've seen, rampant joblessness is an affront to the very idea that persons are created in the image of God and called to be in community with each other and the Divine; involuntary joblessness transgresses the moral order of the universe. In King's view, then, striving to secure the full-employment/right-to-work agenda is one of the ways in which we respect human dignity and move toward the realization of the beloved community. Accordingly, involuntary joblessness is not only a serious social problem, but, equally important, it's also a theological issue. We're under a divine mandate to organize our lives in such a way that we immediately and totally eradicate economic marginality.

In contrast to King, theological premises play no role in either Darity's or Harvey's job guarantee proposals. Yet, they clearly believe that it's wrong or indecent to allow fellow human beings to be slammed by economic forces over which they have no control—forces that stem from the chronic job gap that characterizes the U.S. economy and, if left unchecked, results in elevated levels of joblessness. Put somewhat differently, Darity and Harvey advance what Helen Lachs Ginsburg calls a "humanistic concept of full employment." This concept finds expression in Roosevelt's economic bill of rights, the United Nations Charter, Article 23 of the Universal Declaration of Human Rights, and the Humphrey-Hawkins bill. Ginsburg describes the "humanistic concept of full employment" as follows:

> In this tradition, full employment is explicitly or implicitly considered an aspect of human welfare that includes but goes beyond the welfare state's cash transfers and provision of services. It stresses that greater utilization of human and other resources means rising living standards; and, with some exceptions—for example, women in earlier conceptions—this approach leaves out no individual or group.[1]

And she continues:

> This humanistic concept of full employment recognizes the social as well as the economic role of work and the havoc that ensues when unemployment runs rampant. It is no accident that efforts to promulgate full employment as an overriding goal flourished while embers of World War II still burned, and in that war's aftermath. Full employment was considered a necessary ingredient in the recipe for a just and peaceful world.[2]

King, of course, knew full well that the full-employment/right-to-work agenda was absolutely central to human welfare, and that it was "a necessary ingredient" for the realization of his conception of the beloved community. Yet, as I've mentioned, the ultimate grounds for his response to the havoc of joblessness—as

1. Ginsburg, "Humanistic Concept of Full Employment," 119.
2. Ibid.

well as the call to be concerned about human welfare—are theological in nature. But here's the point that bears emphasis here: that it is possible for people to arrive at the same conclusion, despite starting from different premises, suggests that there is considerable potential for building a broad cross section of support for securing full employment and the right to work. Bringing King into conversation with Darity and Harvey, then, provides evidence that our agreement does not have to go "all the way down" in order for us to arrive at the consensus that what we need is a strategy of direct job creation to eradicate involuntary joblessness.

Fourth, and closely related to the forgoing, this study suggests that our government is currently violating the human rights of millions of jobless persons. It must be emphasized that King, Darity, and Harvey all agree that the government has a moral duty to assure decent work for all, and that this is not simply a matter of discretionary public policy. And with regard to the economic prerequisites of the beloved community, the government's failure to secure full employment and the right to work is particularly egregious because, as Darity and Harvey illustrate, we have the necessary means. There's simply no justification for continuing to allow so many persons to remain stuck in the mire of joblessness, and again, to do so is especially galling when our collective pocketbook is more than deep enough to end this madness. It is imperative, then, that those who seek to bring King's beloved community into fruition use the language of human rights to couch their demand for decent jobs for all. Policy elites must be forced to account for their insistent pursuit of policies that violate the human rights of the jobless. As Harvey points out, it's an established principle of international human rights law and U.S. constitutional law that majorities cannot properly refuse to respect the human rights of minorities:

> If access to useful and remunerative work is indeed a
> human right, then the fact that entrenched political

interests have the power to block initiatives to secure the right cannot be regarded as creating a license to accept that outcome. It is a basic principle of international human rights law (as it is of United States constitutional law) that even a democratically elected legislature, representing the perceived interests of a majority of a nation's population, may not properly refuse to recognize the human rights of a disadvantaged minority group.[3]

He goes on to say that

> A white majority cannot properly refuse to protect the human rights of a nonwhite minority, even if the political process from which the majority derives its putative authority is open to both whites and nonwhites on equal terms. Similarly, if unemployed individuals really are entitled to protection of their right to employment, then even a democratically elected legislature may not properly decide that it is unnecessary or inconvenient to take steps to secure the right.[4]

But all of this underscores a fifth lesson and a point that King himself definitely understood: ultimately, it will take a mass movement to secure genuine full employment and the right to work; it will take people power to translate King's economic bill of rights from words into deeds. King knew that powerful social forces would fiercely resist any and all attempts to change the rules of the game, to shake up the system to such an extent that attending to the needs of the least of these would jump to the top of the nation's to-do list. He was acutely aware of the social and political challenges that stood in the way of securing full employment and the right to work. Thus, at the time of his assassination, he sought to bring an army of the economically deprived to Washington in order to dramatize—and to force policymakers to deal with—the joblessness and poverty that afflicted millions of Americans. He knew

3. Harvey, *Securing the Right to Employment*, 113–14.
4. Ibid., 114.

that wiping out joblessness and all the nasty stuff that goes along with it would require organizing the disorganized—the jobless, the poor, and the economically, politically, and socially marginalized. Until and unless such organizing occurs, King would reminds us, it is highly unlikely that the nation will respond affirmatively to his call for an economic bill of rights; it is highly unlikely, in the absence of a grassroots campaign focused on socioeconomic justice, that the economic prerequisites of the beloved community will ever be realized.

A Way Out

Yet, the fact of the matter is that we aren't destined to live with social, political, and economic arrangements that tolerate involuntary joblessness. We are not destined to have a détente with the social and human wreckage that is inevitably spawned or exacerbated by joblessness—the crime, the lost earnings, the family disruption, the forgone output of goods and services, the increased levels of mental and physical ailments, and the withering of self-esteem. If this study has showed anything, it has shown, I hope, that we have it within our power—that our financial resources are capacious enough—to immediately begin the process of implementing a strategy of direct job creation that brings to fruition the full-employment/right-to-work agenda that constitutes the economic bedrock of King's beloved community. Granted, the misery that accompanies joblessness has the potential to make things look bleak, to make it seem as if there is no way out. But this study, I believe, challenges the pessimism that is inevitably evoked by rampant economic insecurity. If it tells us anything, may it be this: there *is* a way out of no way.

Bibliography

Beveridge, William. *Full Employment in a Free Society*. London: George Allen, 1945.

Birch, Bruce C., and Larry L. Rasmussen. *The Bible and Ethics in the Christian Life*. Rev. ed. Minneapolis: Fortress, 1989.

Bivens, Josh. *Failure by Design: The Story Behind America's Broken Economy*. Ithaca: Cornell University Press, 2011.

Clark, John M., et al. *National and International Measures for Full Employment*. New York: United Nations Department of Economic Affairs, 1949.

Congressional Budget Office. *The Budget and Economic Outlook: Fiscal Years 2010–2020*. Washington, DC: Government Printing Office, 2010.

Darity, William A., Jr. "A Direct Route to Full Employment." *Review of Black Political Economy* 37 (2010) 179–81.

———. "From Here to Full Employment." Samuel Z. Westerfield Address, January 7, 2012, Chicago, Illinois, http://fds.duke.edu/db/attachment/1958.

———. "Insuring Permanent Full Employment." Prepared statement given to the Congressional Black Caucus Deficit Commission, January 28, 2011, http://news.sanford.duke.edu/sites/news.sanford.duke.edu/files/documents/Insuring_permanent_full_employment.pdf.

Davidson, Paul. *The Keynes Solution: The Path to Global Economic Prosperity*. New York: St. Martin's, 2009.

Ginsburg, Helen Lachs. "A Humanistic Concept of Full Employment Transcends the Welfare State." In *Commitment to Full Employment: The Economics and Social Policy of William S. Vickrey*, edited by Aaron W. Warner, Matthew Forstater, and Sumner M. Rosen, 118–24. Armonk, NY: M. E. Sharpe, 2000.

Hansen, Drew D. *The Dream: Martin Luther King, Jr., and the Speech that Inspired a Nation*. New York: HarperCollins, 2002.

Harvey, Philip. "Back to Work: A Public Jobs Proposal for Economic Recovery." Dēmos Policy Brief, 2011, http://www.philipharvey.info/BackToWork.pdf.

————. "Benchmarking the Right to Work." In *Economic Rights: Conceptual, Measurement, and Policy Issues,* edited by Shareen Hertel et al., 115–42. Cambridge: Cambridge University Press, 2007.

————. "Combatting Joblessness: An Analysis of the Principal Strategies that Have Influenced the Development of American Employment and Social Welfare Law during the Twentieth Century." *Berkeley Journal of Employment and Labor Law* 21 (2000) 677–758.

————. "Funding a Job Guarantee." *International Journal of Environment, Workplace and Employment* 2 (2006) 114–29.

————. "Human Rights and Economic Policy Discourse: Taking Economic and Social Rights Seriously." *Columbia Human Rights and Law Review* 33 (2002) 364–471.

————. *Securing the Right to Employment: Social Welfare and the Unemployed in the United States.* Princeton: Princeton University Press, 1989.

————. "Securing the Right to Work at the State or Local Level with a Direct Job Creation Program." http://www.philipharvey.info/securing.pdf.

————. "Why Is the Right to Work So Hard to Secure?" In *The State of Economic and Social Rights: A Global Overview,* edited by Lanse Minkler, 135–74.Cambridge: Cambridge University Press, 2013.

Honey, Michael, ed. *"All Labor Has Dignity."* Boston: Beacon, 2011.

Jackson, Thomas F. *From Civil Rights to Human Rights: Martin Luther King, Jr., and the Struggle for Economic Justice.* Philadelphia: University of Pennsylvania Press, 2007.

King, Martin Luther, Jr. *Where Do We Go from Here: Chaos or Community?* 1967. Reprint, Eugene, OR: Wipf & Stock, 2001.

Lee, Hak Joon. *The Great World House: Martin Luther King, Jr. and Global Ethics.* Cleveland: Pilgrim, 2011.

Long, Michael G. *Against Us, but For Us: Martin Luther King, Jr. and the State.* Macon, GA: Mercer University Press, 2002.

Marcus, Alexis, et al. "An Economic Bill of Rights." *The Review of Black Political Economy* 3.1 (1972) 1–41.

Mucciaroni, Gary. *The Political Failure of Employment Policy, 1945–1982.* Pittsburgh: University of Pittsburgh Press, 1990.

National Resources Planning Board. *Post-war Planning: Full Employment, Security, Building America.* Washington, DC: NRPB, 1942.

Pager, Devah. *Marked: Race, Crime and Finding Work in an Era of Mass Incarceration.* Chicago: University of Chicago Press, 2007.

Paris, Peter J. *Black Religious Leaders: Conflict in Unity.* 2nd ed. Louisville: Westminster John Knox, 1991.

Peck, Don. *Pinched: How the Great Recession Has Narrowed Our Futures and What We Can Do About It.* New York: Crown, 2011.

Pew Economic Policy Group, Fiscal Analysis Initiative. "Addendum—A Year or More: The High Cost of Long-Term Unemployment." May 2012, http:// www.pewtrusts.org/uploadedFiles/wwwpewtrustsorg/Reports/Fiscal_ Analysis/Addendum_Long-Term_Unemployment_May2012.pdf.

———. "A Year or More: The High Cost of Long-Term Unemployment." April 2010, http://www.pewtrusts.org/uploadedFiles/wwwpewtrustsorg/Reports/Economic_Mobility/PEW-Unemployment%20Final.pdf.

Pfeffer, Paula F. A. *Philip Randolph, Pioneer of the Civil Rights Movement*. Baton Rouge: Louisiana State University Press, 1990.

Quigley, William P. *Ending Poverty as We Know It: Guaranteeing a Right to a Job at a Living Wage*. Philadelphia: Temple University Press, 2003.

Rose, Nancy E. *Put to Work: The WPA and Public Employment in the Great Depression*. 2nd ed. New York: Monthly Review, 2009.

Santoni, G. J. "The Employment Act of 1946: Some History Notes." Federal Reserve Bank of St. Louis, November 1986, http://research.stlouisfed.org/publications/review/86/11/Employment_Nov1986.pdf.

Siegel, Richard. *Employment and Human Rights: The International Dimension*. Philadelphia: University of Pennsylvania Press, 1993.

Sunstein, Cass R. *The Second Bill of Rights: FDR's Unfinished Revolution and Why We Need It More than Ever*. New York: Basic Books, 2004.

U.S. Congress. *Economic Security Act of 1935: Hearings on H.R. 4120*, January 21–February 12, Before the Committee on Ways and Means, 74th Congress 23–25 (1935).

Washington, James M., editor. *A Testament of Hope: The Essential Writings and Speeches of Martin Luther King, Jr.* New York: HarperCollins, 1991.

Weir, Margaret. *Politics and Jobs: The Boundaries of Employment Policy in the United States*. Princeton: Princeton University Press, 1992.